African Wax Print

A Textile Journey

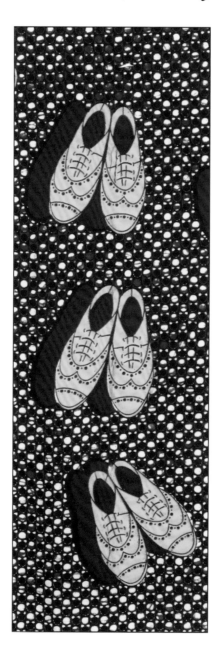

Published by Words and Pixels
www.wordsandpixels.co.uk

Front cover image: Fabric vendor, Koforidua, Ghana

Back cover image: Daboya, Ghana

African Wax Print

A Textile Journey

Magie Relph & Robert Irwin

Published by Words and Pixels
www.wordsandpixels.co.uk

For The African Fabric Shop
www.africanfabric.co.uk

ISBN 978-0-9566982-0-9

First published in the United Kingdom by Words and Pixels
19 Hebble Mount, Meltham, Holmfirth, HD9 4HG United Kingdom
www.wordsandpixels.co.uk

Design: Christopher Lawther, Teamwork Graphics
Copy-editor/proofreader: Katherine James
French translations: Huguette Savoie

Printed by Gemini Press

This book is available from www.africanfabric.co.uk

Contents

Introducing African wax print fabric

The journey begins

Utter the phrase 'African fabric' and what do you imagine? Chances are, you'll see an image of an African woman.

She could be a market trader, sitting in the dust with her pile of tomatoes and onions in front of the mud-brick mosque of Djenne in Mali. Maybe she's a *Nana Benz*, a big, buxom fabric entrepreneur in the grand *marché* in Lomé, the fetish-fixated capital of Togo. Or even a sauntering, seductive fashion model, swirling down the catwalk in Paris, London or New York.

Aside from the colour of their skin, what tells us that all of these women, similar but different, are African? What visual clue virtually defines their African-ness?

For the vegetable vendor in Djenne, it's her simple cotton wrap-around, perhaps twinned with a second wrapper to strap her baby onto her back. For Nana Benz, it's an elaborately tailored, fitted and ruffled three-piece suit, complete with matching head-tie. For the high-fashion model, it's the latest cutting-edge design – bold, bright and beautiful.

From Mali to Manhattan, from market stall to *haute couture*, the common denominator for all of these women and their costumes is the cloth that has dominated the African fabric market for over a century. It's the colourful, vibrant and distinctive African wax print.

So what exactly is African wax print? Where does it come from? What does it mean in the context of Africa's diverse textile heritage? How do Africans use wax print in Africa? And how is it used in the wider world, in the UK, Europe and America;

by Africans and non-Africans; and by the many designers, quilters and textile artists who are inspired by Africa and its textiles?

To find out, let's take a journey, from the origins of wax print in 19th-century Europe to the markets of West Africa and beyond. Along the way, we'll see wax print being worn, cut up, stitched, quilted, cherished and enjoyed.

So welcome aboard. Next stop … Africa (with a slight detour via Java, Holland and England).

Where to first? You decide

Every journey has to begin somewhere, so we start with the history and development of wax print. It's a fascinating and surprising story. But maybe you're more interested in wax print design or how these fabrics are used in Africa and beyond. That's just fine: you can start where you like. After all, it's your journey.

Bon voyage

Telling the story

When we started this project, we already knew quite a bit about African wax print. Over the years we've collected many books and articles. To those we've added information tracked down in cyberspace, plus notebooks full of anecdotes recorded from conversations in England and Africa.

Regarding dates, names and the like, we've done our best to be precise. But we must be honest: as our pile of facts, figures and sources got bigger, we found many contradictions and gaps.

Image courtesy of A Brunnschweiler & Co.

At first, we (mainly Bob) panicked and tried to resolve them. Then, we (mainly Magie) said, 'Get real.'

We thought about you, our readers. We realised that most of you are not scholars. You are textile artists, stitchers, weavers, spinners, dyers and embroiderers – quite simply, the community of textile lovers.

At that point, we said, 'Wait.'

We're not writing the definitive, last words on the subject of African wax print. That job is for academics. All we're doing is telling you a story. It's as accurate as we can make it. We hope it inspires you as much as the fabrics do.

Waiting for the bus,
Sikasso, Mali

A special thanks

Over the years we've spent many hours chatting with our friend Paul McDonough of A Brunnschweiler & Co. Paul has been in the wax print business for 45 years, 19 of them either living in Africa or travelling somewhere on the dusty, rutted roads between Freetown, Lomé and Kinshasa.

Thank you, Paul … for generously sharing your time and knowledge, but mostly for your enthusiasm.

Preparing for market,
Djenne, Mali

1 From batik to wax print

The scramble for Africa

Africa is rich in textile traditions. When you think of the continent's sheer size and scale, is it any wonder?

Political Africa has 54 countries. The real Africa, where village and family mean more than artificial boundaries, has thousands of ethnic groups and languages. Africa's people, over a billion of them, adhere to a mix of traditional animist, Islamic and Christian beliefs. Africa's four major time zones cover the vast Congo rainforests, the Sahara, Kalahari and Namib deserts, and three great rivers – the Nile, Congo and Niger. Geographically and culturally, words like 'vast' and 'diverse' are not really big enough for Africa.

To appreciate the scope of Africa's textile heritage, consider just three examples.

In the Musée National in Bamako, Mali, you can see fragments of hand-woven, hand-dyed indigo fabrics that date back to the 12th century. A few kilometres away in the market you can find the same cloth, dyed and woven using the same methods and equipment.

In Ghana and Togo, Ashanti and Ewe master weavers create Kente, the colourful, complex, expensive and absolutely distinctive cloth of kings. Every pattern has a name and every combination a meaning. The only difference between a cloth woven by a man with a mobile phone hanging from his loom and the cloths

African map print, Malawi, 1980s

Makola Market, Accra

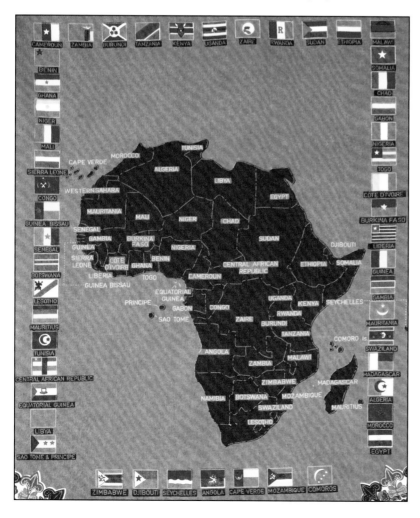

woven generations ago by his forefathers is the weft threads. In modern cloths they are usually rayon. In ancient cloths they were silk, laboriously unravelled from the luxurious fabrics brought by European traders.

In Nigeria, Guinea, Ghana and Mali, dyers use traditional methods of tying, stitching and starch painting to create a resist, before plunging their cloths into vats of frothing, fuming indigo. Their techniques, their patterns and their methods have stayed largely unchanged for centuries.

Flash forward to the turn of the 19th century. In Europe, textile manufacture was being transformed by industrialisation. Cottage weavers were now mill workers. Inventors, innovators and engineers became mill owners. They were the entrepreneurs of their age.

Fatmata Babage, traditional indigo dyer, Endé, Mali

Meanwhile, the scramble for Africa was on. The British, French, Dutch, Spanish, Portuguese, Germans and Italians all sought new colonies where they could sell the output of their steaming factories in exchange for gold, ivory, rubber and slaves.

One industrial product that Europe, and especially England, churned out in abundance, quite literally by the mile, was woven cotton cloth. One particular cloth, for a number of related reasons, seemed destined for Africa. That cloth was *African wax print*.

The Java–Dutch connection

In simple terms, African wax print is an industrialised version of hand-drawn, hand-blocked, hand-dyed batik.

Traditional hand-made batik goes back to 8th-century China and then India, where

creative artisans produced coloured designs on cotton fabrics using a simple wax resist technique. Their tool was a primitive drawing pen made of two sticks tied together with a ball of fibres between to hold the wax.

In the 13th century, the islanders of Java refined this technique. They turned the Indians' crude painting stick into a more sophisticated wax applicator called a *canting* (or *tjanting*). This tool is made up of a copper bowl to hold the hot, melted wax, with a handle and spout for pouring and applying the wax.

Using the *canting*, the Javanese could apply the wax to the fabric with greater precision, so designs became more detailed and complex. Eventually, to make a better resist, they started applying wax to both surfaces of the cloth. For multicoloured designs, each new colour required its own layer of wax resist. The process was very slow and labour intensive, but as batik cloth became more sophisticated, it became so popular that demand always exceeded supply.

Now came the first of several colonial connections, this one in the early 1880s.

Java was the centre of the Dutch East Indies (modern Indonesia). Like most European colonies, it functioned in many ways as the commercial playground of the colonial power, Holland.

In 1830, Holland faced a serious crisis at home. The region of Flanders seceded and joined the new state of Belgium. Unfortunately for the Dutch, Flanders was the site of most of Holland's textile mills. Something had to be done.

In a few short years the enterprising Dutch built three new textile factories in Haarlem. Two of them – the Turkey Red dye works and Previnaire & Co. – eventually joined forces as the Haarlem Cotton Company (in Dutch, *Haarlem Katoen Maatschappijhe* or HKM). This company's innovations and achievements had a direct impact on the Dutch East Indies, Dutch commercial activities in West Africa and ultimately the birth of wax print.

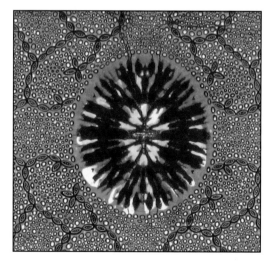

Hand-painted Indonesian batik (top); early English wax prints by Brotherton (middle) and Elson & Neill (bottom)

In its attempt to break into the huge Indonesian batik market, HKM took a gamble. It looked at the painstakingly slow method of drawing batik by hand using the *canting*. 'This is industrialised Europe,' it was reasoned. 'Surely we can speed up the process, making it cheaper and more profitable.'

Copper cap, *Java*

Elmina Castle overlooking the former Gold Coast, modern Ghana

Their new machine was called *La Javanais*.

This new process was called *wax block printing*. Its main advantages over hand-drawn batik were speed and simplicity. Hand-drawn batik requires a separate application of wax for each new colour in the design. Wax block printing requires only one application of wax, followed by a dye dip in the primary colour, usually indigo. Then each additional colour is applied with its own sequence of hand-blockings.

So did the Dutch wax block printing technique produce a successful facsimile of batik? Not to the Javanese! The Dutch batik venture was a failure.

However, the Dutch quickly discovered this was easier said than done. Experiment after experiment failed. They even imported Javanese batik workers, hoping to decipher the secret. Then, in 1854, the Dutch finally did it. Using a modified French plate printing machine coupled with carved wooden blocks bearing the designs, they created their own version of Java batik.

Meanwhile, the Javanese improved their own process by inventing a copper stamp called the *cap* (or *tjap)*. Using this new device to supplement the traditional *canting*, they could apply wax to fabric much more quickly and cheaply. The Javanese kept control of their own batik market, leaving the Dutch to ponder their next move.

Meanwhile in Manchester: the British are coming

The Dutch were not the only European power frantic to develop, produce and above all sell the outputs of their newly mechanised textile mills to their colonies. In the scramble for Africa and markets around the world, if the British weren't out in front, they were never far behind.

The textile industry was a cornerstone of the British Empire. The *triangle of trade* took slaves from West Africa to America, cotton from America to England, and millions of yards of cotton fabric around the world, including to Africa. The north of England and especially Manchester was where it all happened.

Even before the Dutch began exporting their version of batik to West Africa, the British were already leading the world in textile manufacture and innovation. In 1771 Richard Arkwright built the first water-powered cotton mill in Cromford, Derbyshire. In 1783 Scotsman James Bell invented an engraved roller printing machine in Preston, Lancashire.

Then, in 1816 at Newton Bank in Hyde, Greater Manchester, a small workshop produced its first mechanised, roller-printed cotton fabric. It wasn't African wax print as we know it today, but that company would eventually become *A Brunnschweiler & Co.*, makers of ABC, one of the premier wax print brands.

And in Haarlem: African wax print is born

Back in Haarlem, the Dutch were still striving for a mechanised method of making batik that would work. Their perseverance finally paid off when printer JB Previnaire adapted a French banknote printing machine to apply a resin (not wax) resist to both sides of the cloth simultaneously. After dyeing the cloth and washing away the resist, the Dutch had a perfectly acceptable version of Javanese batik. Or so they thought.

Yet again, as Dutch ships sailed east laden with fabrics, the Haarlem textile barons rubbed their hands in glee at the

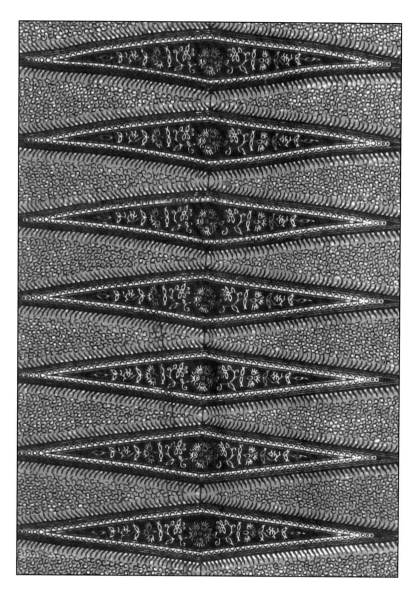

Brazza design wax print by Elson & Neill, inspired by Indonesian Tumpal design

expectation of profit. It didn't come, at least not immediately; and when the money finally did roll in, it was not from Indonesia, but from West Africa.

When the Dutch batiks arrived in Indonesia, they were a failure. Nobody would buy them. The reason had less to do with the designs, which after all copied original Javanese designs, than with the mechanised production method devised by Previnaire.

The problem was the resin. As the resist paste dried on the surface of the fabric, it cracked. Dye seeped through the cracks, giving the fabric a distinct *crackle* effect. 'Rubbish,' said the Indonesian batik aficionados. Once again, the Dutch had a product without a market.

Enter an enterprising Scot – Ebenezer Brown Fleming.

Grafton wax print, influenced by Indonesian designs

A new market emerges: Africa

Ebenezer Brown Fleming, acting as an agent for HKM, had an idea. 'If the Indonesians won't buy our fabrics,' he conjectured, 'maybe the Africans will.' His idea wasn't as crazy as it sounds.

The Dutch were already heavily involved in West Africa, with flourishing trading forts along the Gold Coast, today's Ghana. Also, they regularly recruited African men into the Dutch East Indies Army – some 3,000 between 1855 and 1872.

When these globetrotting African soldiers returned to their villages, they didn't dare come empty-handed. With textiles already an important part of West African culture, they brought the wife back home the perfect gift – hand-made Java batiks.

By 1893 the ladies of the Gold Coast had acquired a taste for these vibrant and colourful fabrics. So when Ebenezer Brown Fleming's first shipment of Dutch-made mechanised batik arrived from Haarlem, it was an instant success.

The Dutch were back on a winner. Their facsimile batiks were called the *Haarlem range* and some of those early designs are still produced today.

As Africa opened up as a new market for this mechanised batik, developments in Holland and England came fast and furious. And who was wheeling and dealing in the thick of the action? None other than the canny Scot – Ebenezer Brown Fleming.

Nobody knows if Brown Fleming ever went to Africa himself, but he certainly made his mark there, and probably his money. Records are either sparse or non-existent, so piecing together his commercial activities isn't easy, and even among serious scholars guesses outnumber hard facts.

Brown Fleming was a Glaswegian, but he came from a Flemish textile family. We do know that he was an agent for Turkey Red printers and HKM, and at some date founded Brown Fleming Ltd, Dyers and Printers of African and Colonial Specialities. Brown Fleming had his finger in two competing pies – one Dutch, one English. Somehow he understood the African market, what was popular and what was not, and his ideas had an influence on both Dutch and English designs. Also, around 1900, he registered some of the original Dutch designs in England. The repercussions of that still rumble on to this day – we return to that later in the story.

Throughout this era, as the Dutch side of the wax print industry developed, a parallel story was unfolding in Manchester.

Genuine English wax print: ABC

Although the selvedges of English wax prints display many brands and logos, the biggest and most enduring has been ABC. In many ways its story encapsulates that of the Industrial Revolution and its connections to the African textile trade.

By the 1800s British firms were diligently producing cotton fabrics for the Empire, including the Gold Coast which became an official colony in 1874. Along with several other Manchester textile mills, Newton Bank in Hyde was owned by three brothers – Joseph, Benjamin and Robert Ashton. By 1830, Newton Bank's five roller machines were printing 3 million yards of fabric a year. While this was an astounding output, it was still a conventional printed fabric.

By 1856 the original Ashton brothers had all died and the business passed to a nephew, Francis William Tinker. To maintain continuity, Tinker adopted his mother's maiden name. As a result, for the next 114 years until 1970, the company's merchant arm was FW Ashton & Co., while the manufacturing arm remained Newton Bank print works.

During this era of England's textile history, invention was the key to success. Every new discovery roared like a tidal wave through the industry.

Consider the dramatic advancements in the technology of dyeing, for example. For centuries, dyers around the world have extracted colour from berries, leaves, bark, insects and shellfish. With the scientific discoveries of the Victorian era, all that changed.

Fabric label for Brotherton of Manchester

St James's Buildings, CPA Headquarters, Manchester

In 1856, chemist Henry Perkins dramatically expanded the colour spectrum for dyeing fabrics when he created the first synthetic dyestuff based on aniline, a by-product of coal tar. In 1878, German chemist Adolf von Baeyer successfully synthesised indigo. Meanwhile in Manchester, after FW Ashton's son James returned from studying chemistry in Germany, Newton Bank became a centre of innovation for textile printing and dyeing.

Even as northern England's mill owners raked in the profits from the 19th-century textile boom, competition from the rest of Europe was fierce. In response, 46 firms (including FW Ashton and Newton Bank print works) amalgamated in 1899 to form the Calico Printers' Association (CPA).

The CPA included textile printers, as well as spinning, weaving and dyeing concerns. Its members produced 85% of Britain's printed fabrics. As a measure of the money involved, look no further than the CPA's head office, the imposing St James's Building in Manchester's Oxford Street. Opened in 1912, it comprises over 1,000 rooms connected by a mile of corridors. At its peak the switchboard handled a million calls a year from traders around the world.

What's in a name? Plenty of confusion

In England, many of the wax print companies were actually made up of two distinct operations. One – the print works, often called the *finisher* – was responsible for production. The other – the *commercial* arm – did the actual selling. It also made sure that the designs and colourways were suitable for wax printing, and had them engraved onto copper rollers.

The wax printer's customers were referred to as merchants, or sometimes *merchant-converters*. Many of them created their own designs and gave them, along with the unprinted cotton (called *grey cloth*), to the print works. From there, full rolls of wax print, usually 120 yards long, went to the *makers-up*. These companies checked for flaws, cut the fabric into selling lengths (typically 6 or 12 yards), then labelled and baled them for export. The merchants usually sold the fabric to intermediary companies called *shippers*, who then sold the goods on, either *to* or *in* Africa.

The company we now know as A Brunnschweiler & Co. of Hyde, Greater Manchester, was initially made up of a print works – Newton Bank – and its commercial arm – FW Ashton & Co.

Newton Bank printed for various merchants, such as HJ Barrett, Joseph Bridge, Elson & Neill, Grafton Africa and Logan Muckelt. In the early days, these were the names that appeared on the selvedge.

The merchants' customers – the shippers – included GB Ollivant, J Holt, UAC and two other significant firms: Paterson Zochonis, a small West African trading company that eventually became PZ Cussons, maker of English Leather soaps; and a little-known Swiss company trading in West Africa – A Brunnschweiler & Co.

To further confuse matters, A Brunnschweiler & Co. is often referred to by its initials – ABC – which today is the brand logo it prints on the selvedge of its fabrics.

In Holland, PF van Vlissingen & Co., following a series of mergers and acquisitions, eventually became Vlisco, which today is the premier Dutch brand of wax print.

In 1902, the Broad Oak print works in Accrington made England's first non-mechanised, hand-blocked wax print. Matching sets of hand-cut wooden blocks were used to apply the same wax resist pattern to both sides of the fabric. One set of blocks was minutely smaller than the other, which accounted for a slight shrinkage after stamping the first side of the fabric.

Newton Bank made its first hand-blocked wax print around 1906, followed quickly by other firms: Horridge & Cornell in Bury, BF Crompton in Manchester, Astbury & Pickford in Oldham, Marple Printing in Marple, and United Turkey Red in Glasgow.

While hand-blocking produced an excellent, marketable product, the process was slow. Mechanisation was the key. Records are sketchy, but an engraving book from Grafton Africa, the merchant arm of Broad Oak, records the first use of duplex wax printing rollers in 1909–10.

Workers in the wax printing machine room, A Brunnschweiler & Co

ABC billboard, Accra, 1980s (below)

ABC's new man in Africa

It was a dreary winter afternoon in Manchester. A Friday in 1971, ten minutes to five. The managing director called me into his office. I was young and I'd only been with the company a few years. 'What could the MD possibly want with me?' I thought.

Glancing at his watch, he got straight to the point. 'Our technical director in Lagos just resigned. How do you feel about taking his place?'

'How long have I got to decide?' I asked.

The MD checked his watch again. 'My train leaves in eight minutes.'

'Give me two months to get married and I'll go,' I said. We shook hands and the MD left for the station.

Two months later, a day after celebrating my 25th birthday, my wife and I boarded a BOAC VC10 bound for Lagos. For the next seven years, we called Nigeria's biggest, brashest city 'home' and I was one of just six ABC men in Africa.

Paul McDonough, A Brunnschweiler & Co.
Photographed in Kinshasa, 1989

This mechanised technology reached Newton Bank around 1920. Suddenly, the company could print 500 yards of fabric at a time, compared with 20 yards by hand-blocking. At this point, the engraved copper rollers were used only to apply the resist before dyeing. Illuminating colours were still hand-blocked.

In the 1930s, BF Crompton developed a mechanical fitting machine which applied the illuminating colours continuously using engraved copper rollers – a major breakthrough for speed and productivity. However, because aligning the colours on both sides of the fabric was difficult, the Crompton machine was only used for simple designs. Hand-blocking was still used for more complicated designs.

Following an understandable decline during the Second World War, by the 1950s Africa's appetite for wax print was insatiable. Newton Bank alone was printing 8 million yards a year; by 1960–61, that figure was 25 million yards.

The 1960s was a decade of massive change and high hopes for Africa, as the European colonial powers, mainly Britain and France, bowed to political pressure and granted independence to their African possessions.

Ghana was the first, in 1957, and by 1968 it was the largest single market for English wax print. Meanwhile, oil was discovered in the Niger delta. Nigeria, Africa's most populous new nation, was suddenly booming. And Nigeria, like the rest of West Africa, bought an awful lot of wax print fabric.

During this period the English companies continued to jostle for market share. In 1959, the CPA bought a modest and little-known Swiss company – *A Brunnschweiler & Co.*, which had an established trading network in Africa. That company's initials would eventually emerge as the premier brand of English wax: ABC.

In 1968 the CPA merged with English Sewing to trade as English Calico, which in 1973 became Tootal, one of English Sewing's existing and best-known brands. Today, Brunnschweiler still designs the ABC brand of wax print at Newton Bank in Manchester, although between 2005 and 2007 it gradually moved production to Ghana.

The post-independence era saw other textile factories, some producing wax print, spring up in Ghana, Nigeria, Senegal, Côte d'Ivoire and Zaire. Some were successful, some were not.

In Ghana, GTP (a subsidiary of Vlisco) and ATL (Akosombo Textiles Ltd, linked to Brunnschweiler) are still going strong. Other brands, some of which have come and gone, include Printex, ERG, Sonitextil, Uniwax and ICODL. In Dakar, Société Tientre et Blanchissement (SOTIBA), once heavily subsidised by the French government to create a monopoly supplier in the region, still survives, despite its ups and downs and several international owners.

Genuine Dutch wax print: Vlisco

Just as Brunnschweiler turned ABC into the premier English brand, its main competitor did the same in Holland. Today, the Vlisco company and brand are synonymous in Africa with top-quality Dutch wax print.

Vlisco was founded in 1846 in Helmond by PF van Vlissingen and competed with the established Dutch textile companies in Haarlem. Initially, van Vlissingen & Co. produced fabrics for the domestic market, as well as hand-blocked batiks for the tough Dutch East Indies market. However, looking for a new outlet for its products, in 1876 the company began exporting to West Africa, primarily to the receptive markets of the Gold Coast.

1906 saw the first Dutch successful mechanised wax printing, by HKM in Haarlem. Van Vlissingen followed suit in 1910, and from the 1920s they were industry leaders in design, quality and marketing acumen.

In 1929, partly in an effort to stimulate a floundering domestic market, the company adopted a new type of fabric called *fancy print*, which featured novelty designs and images. This concept continues to this day in the African market.

Since its early days, van Vlissingen has been an innovator in both design and technology, including dyestuffs. From the 1930s its distribution in Africa was managed by a company called UAC, which later became part of Unilever. A series of mergers and acquisitions through the 1960s led to the emergence in 1970 of a new company, image and brand: *Vlisco*.

14,000 miles of wax print

In 2010, just two European wax print companies are still in business – ABC in England and Vlisco in Holland. Only Vlisco still produces in Europe. ABC moved production to its Ghana factory in 2007, although the design studio is still in Manchester. Today, the competition from cheap Chinese counterfeits is crippling. Eventually, it may kill the industry entirely.

Looking back to wax print in its heyday, we see a very different picture. Back then, wax print was big business – *very* big business. The scale and the numbers really were staggering.

In the early 1960s, the Newton Bank print works in Manchester (now ABC) sold 24 million yards of wax print a year, virtually all of it to Africa. That's over 14,000 miles of fabric, enough to stretch from Manchester to Accra and back again – twice!

In 1966, three print works – Newton Bank, Vlisco in Holland and Hohlenstein in Switzerland – sold a combined 50 million yards of wax print.

Consider ABC's *Classic Collection* of 28 wax print designs – those with the greatest staying power. Eighteen have sold over 1 million yards each – and counting. The two most popular, *Dice* and *New Fine Trail*, have each sold 25 million yards so far, and they are still in production.

By any measure – yardage, money or just cultural impact – that's a lot of fabric.

Dutch fabric label for English client, 1958

Today, as part of Actis, Vlisco is the last company still producing wax print in Europe.

The price of success: 5 cents

Looking back from the recession-riddled 21st century, it's sometimes hard to comprehend the yardage and money involved when the wax print industry was at its peak. Paul McDonough of A Brunnschweiler & Co. recalls a sales junket in the 1980s.

In those days, getting wax print into the shops and market stalls of Africa was more than just a selling job. We had to know our markets and every country was different. Success depended on choosing the perfect combination of designs and colourations.

I was in Monrovia, capital of Liberia, working on a deal. I'd been in the business a while by then, so my product selection was pretty good. The only stumbling block was price and my customer, a big player in the West African textile market, was as tough as they come. $1.85 a yard was his final offer. I was after $1.90.

After several days at loggerheads, my time was up and – still negotiating – we headed for the airport. Six fruitless hours later, deflated by the heat, humidity and haggling, I said good-bye and turned for the departure gate.

Suddenly, my adversary extended his hand. I had my 5 cents. It was worth every drop of sweat I'd lost. The order was for 2 million yards.

Enter the dragon: the Chinese in Africa

Modern, independent, 21st-century Africa is a very different place from its post-colonial equivalent. In 1960 you would never have found an excellent Chinese restaurant, run by Chinese for Chinese, in a place like Kumasi, the old Ashanti capital of Ghana. Today, you can.

All across Africa, the Chinese dragon has landed and it's definitely *not* hiding. The numbers for 2010 are astounding: 750,000 Chinese live and work in Africa, contributing to over $100 billion in African–Chinese trade. From agriculture to construction and mining to manufacturing, wherever there are deals to make, the Chinese are making them. The textile industry is no exception.

Probably the most prominent Chinese player in the African textile market is the Cha Group. Founded in 1949 by Cha Chi Ming in Hong Kong, today Cha Textiles is big in Africa – very big.

Across its companies, Cha employs 18,000 people in Africa. Its dyeing and printing capacity is 213 million metres per year. Cha either manufactures or distributes in Nigeria, Ghana, Côte d'Ivoire, Benin, Togo, Niger and the Congo. In Nigeria alone it owns four major textile companies – United Nigerian Textiles, Zamfara Textiles, Funtua Textiles and Qualitex. In Ghana it owns Akosombo Textiles (ATL), one of Africa's most successful wax print producers.

Since 1992 Cha has owned an even more important part of African and British textile heritage: none other than A Brunnschweiler & Co. and its premier brand, ABC Wax.

For more than a decade, Cha swam against the tide and kept wax print production going in Manchester. However, by 2005 the writing was on the wall for Newton Bank. As the production and transport costs soared, Cha had no other choice. It began the expensive two-year process of moving an entire wax print factory closer to the market, to its affiliated factory in Akosombo, Ghana.

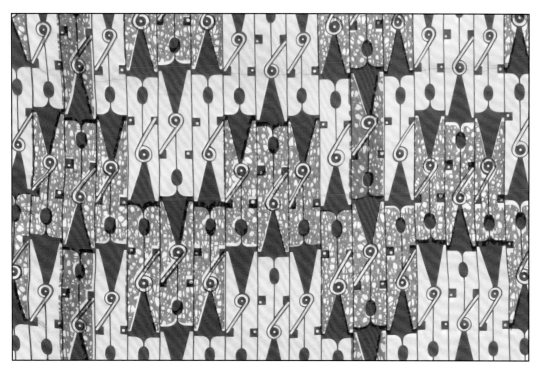

Chinese wax print by Hitarget (top) and early Made-in-Ghana ABC wax print, 2007

Today, while the Newton Bank site may be quiet, the design studio is as busy as ever. Working from the archive of 35,000 designs, some dating back to 1909, augmented by constant feedback from their customers in Africa, ABC designers create up to 250 new wax print designs a year. There's only one difference: now the selvedge reads *Made in Ghana*.

Enter another dragon: the black market

It is Easter 2009. We are stuck in traffic in Accra (what else is new?) with our shipping agent en route to Kotoka International Airport.

We are listening to a phone-in show on Radio Ghana when we hear a voice we know. The speaker is Steve Dutton, marketing manager of Akosombo Textiles (ATL), sister company to A Brunnschweiler & Co. and one of Ghana's leading textile weavers and printers. He is talking about Ghana's booming black market for fabrics.

(The following figures are estimates only.) According to the BBC, Ghana buys over 150 million yards of wax print a year. That's about $250 million worth of cloth. Only 25% of this fabric is actually made in Ghana, by companies that employ Ghanaian workers, like ATL and GTP.

A comparatively small slice of the market goes to prestige, imported wax prints, those still designed and produced by Vlisco in Holland and, until 2007, by ABC in England. Another slice goes to Uniwax from Côte d'Ivoire. The remainder, almost $190 million worth of fabric, comes from China.

Chinese facsimile wax print (top), labelled Auden, Manchester

Target *or* Record Disc, *a classic wax print design*

Some, but not much, of this Chinese fabric is legitimate. In other words, the designs are *not* stolen from other companies and the fabrics are legally imported into Ghana, with tax and duty of about 20% paid to the Ghana exchequer. Every remaining yard of fabric that enters Ghana is illegal, a black market commodity. From the industrial sweatshops of China, it arrives in the duty-free port of Lomé in neighbouring Togo. From there, it is smuggled by truck across the border into Ghana.

This trade in black market fabrics seems almost unstoppable. When you look at the numbers, is it any wonder? The prices quoted here will have changed since we recorded them in Accra in January 2010, but they are a good starting point.

Imagine you are a Ghanaian consumer. Like most of your neighbours, you earn about $2 per day. You are in the Makola market and you have a choice: genuine Dutch wax print, made in Holland – $75 for a 6 yard length; Ghanaian wax print from ATL or GTP – about $16–$23; legitimately imported Chinese wax print – $10. Or a smuggled, black market copy from China – as low as $5, just over twice your daily wage.

Now, look at your outgoings. Fuel is up. Rice is up. In fact, everything is up. The only thing not up is smuggled Chinese fabric. It's a no-brainer. You buy what you can afford, the black market copy.

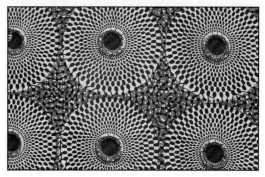

So, what have you bought? Quite honestly, the fakes are easy to spot. The cotton itself is very poor quality, loosely woven and crudely finished. It isn't a genuine wax print at all, but a copy – referred to locally as a *fancy print*. This isn't bad in itself. There are some very good-quality fancy prints on the market. But your Chinese copy is not one of them. The design and colours are misaligned. Above all, compared with a genuine wax print, the black market copy is dull and lifeless. In short, you've bought a very poor-quality fabric. Unfortunately, though, this is all you can afford.

At this point, Steve Dutton (ATL) takes up the tale. He told the Ghana *Daily Graphic* that his company is not really concerned with foreign-made textiles imported through legitimate channels. Far from it.

A blanket ban on imports 'does not give the consumer the right of choice', he said, 'and we also believe that it is not everybody who can afford every textile on the market because of the prices. But let us have fair competition by paying our taxes' – unlike, we need hardly add, the black marketeers.

Who, then, are the losers to this nefarious trade?

First, the Ghanaian treasury. The smugglers do not pay tax or duty as they cross the border. Also, market traders and retail shops do not pay VAT to the government on black market goods they have bought from the smugglers.

Second, the legitimate brands like Vlisco, ABC and ATL. These companies invest heavily in their own unique designs. Like any intellectual property, these designs are registered and protected by copyright laws. Some designs are instantly popular and profitable. However, the market is fickle and some designs just don't sell. When this happens, the companies have to absorb the loss.

Compare this with the black market. The forgers don't waste their money copying unpopular designs. They watch the market carefully and when they spot a winning design, they grab it. In a matter of weeks their cheap copies, smuggled into Ghana via Togo, are for sale in Makola market.

Third, the Ghanaian economy. The *Daily Graphic* put the loss at $31 million in 2003, the most recent year quoted.

Fourth, arguably the biggest losers of all are the Ghanaian people. In January 2010 the textile industry in Ghana employed only 3,000 workers, compared with a peak of 25,000 in the 1970s. In addition, every penny that is not paid to the treasury in duty, VAT, corporate or income tax, is money that cannot be spent on the healthcare, education and infrastructure that the people need.

Now, the ultimate blow. On 2 February 2010, we picked up the *Daily Graphic* in Accra to read this shock headline: 'Textile industry faces gloomy future'. Akosombo Textiles, the largest textile company in the country, sent home two-thirds of its workforce, some 1,600 employees.

The immediate cause for the shutdown and layoff was a shortage of fuel to run the factory. But lurking in the background was

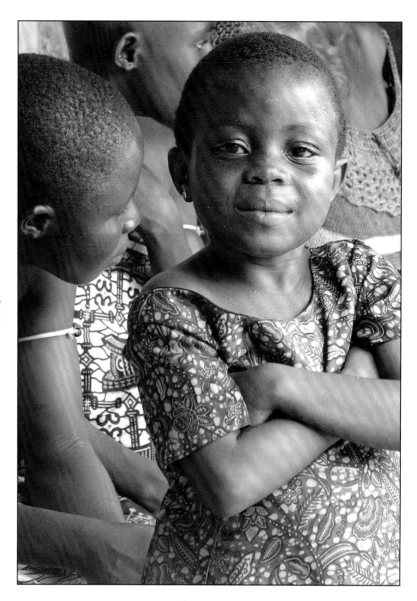

a deeper problem, the massively profitable and virtually unrestrained black market.

So far, we've only described Ghana, but the textile industry is threatened elsewhere too. Nigeria is Africa's second largest textile producer, after Egypt. The most recent figures available are just as grim as those for Ghana: in 2007–08, almost 100 of Nigeria's 250 textile factories closed, throwing more than 13,000 people out of work. There are many contributing factors, including the declining value of the Nigerian currency, the high cost of fuel (even though Nigeria is a leading oil producer), lack of capital investment and, of course, the black market.

In the face of these difficulties, the future of African wax print looks uncertain. The fabric markets of West Africa are definitely changing, maybe for ever.

Young girl, Odumasi, Ghana. Will wax print survive for the next generation?

2 The making of African wax print

The art of perfect imperfection

Examine most African wax prints and you'll instantly recognise the elements that set this unique fabric apart from most other factory-produced textiles.

- The colours: bright, brash and unusual combinations that can make you wonder if the designers have ever seen a colour wheel.

- The designs: sometimes big and bold, sometimes delicate and subtle, but *always* printed on both sides of the fabric. Some designs date back to the origins of the African textile trade in the 1900s, others are bang up to date, depicting 21st-century technologies like computers and mobile phones.

- Most characteristic of all, the two distinct irregularities of African wax print: a slight misalignment of colour and design, plus the distinctive *crackle* effect. Taken together, these two irregularities give to wax print what we might call its *perfect imperfection*.

So how do manufacturers like ABC achieve the unique qualities that define African wax print fabrics? Read on, for all will be revealed – almost. The rest remains obscured by the dark shadows of industrial espionage. In other words, it's a secret.

From the days of Ebenezer Brown Fleming and FW Ashton, many English and Dutch companies competed ferociously for the African wax print trade. Their goal was market dominance and profit. Their weapon was innovation.

The companies were locked in a perpetual battle to invent new processes, speed up production, improve quality and above all

The perfect imperfection: both classic and modern designs show wax print's trademark crackle effect

create new designs for their discerning customers, the ladies of West Africa.

Even today, the few remaining companies keep many of the technical aspects of wax print production hidden behind their locked factory gates.

We've been lucky, though. Over the years we've enjoyed the occasional glimpse behind the gates of both ABC in England and ATL in Ghana. We've seen the design teams manipulating colour and image using the latest computer graphics software. We've seen the output of their creativity, metre after metre of wax print fabric coming off the printing lines. And, we've even seen some, but not all, of the bits in between.

Achieving the look of perfect imperfection that makes African wax print fabric unique isn't easy.

First of all, the printing process and technology date back to the 19th century, a period of industrial and textile invention, especially in England. Today, even with modern machinery and computers, many aspects of wax print production seem more Dickensian than high-tech.

Second, the perfect imperfections that define wax print did not result from clever design or manufacturing innovation. They were accidents. As any artist will tell you, it's almost impossible to reproduce an accident – which in many ways is what the wax print process is all about.

Wax print production

Put simply, African wax print is a mechanised version of batik, which is a method of resist dyeing. The concept of resist dyeing is easy to grasp.

The artist paints the surface of the fabric with a resist substance, which in the case of batik is wax. When the fabric is immersed in the dye vat, the wax coating prevents the dye from colouring the fabric. Only the unwaxed areas of the fabric will be dyed.

Wash away the wax resist and the design is revealed. For more complex designs, the artist will apply many layers of wax, each followed by its own dye dip.

Fabric dyers have been using variations of this resist technique for centuries in many regions of the world. Java, the spiritual home of batik, is just one. Resist dyeing, especially with indigo, also has a long history in West Africa.

In the 19th century, English and Dutch textile barons took this simple resist process a step further by doing what they did best: they invented a machine that would do it faster and cheaper. African wax print was born.

The methods seen in modern-day wax print production at ABC and ATL are not so very different from those used at FW Ashton's Newton Bank print works at the turn of the 20th century.

This mechanised batik process begins with the resist itself. Surprisingly, the resist is not

The perfect imperfection: slight misalignment of colour and design

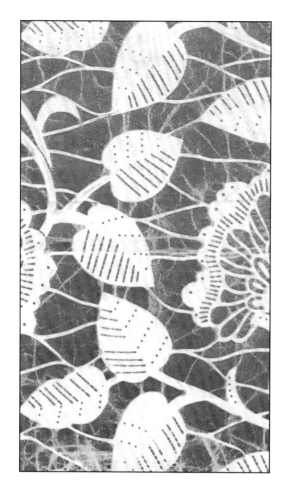

The wax print process (clockwise from top left): resin resist applied; after indigo dyeing, resist partially removed; supplementary colours applied by hand-block, screen or engraved roller; finished wax print

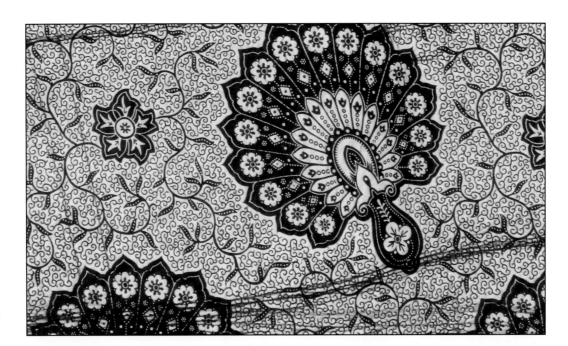

Deliberate crackle effect applied to wax print

wax, as the name *wax print* implies. Exact recipes vary slightly and remain secret, but we do know that the most important ingredient is a tree resin.

Before it can be used, the resin must be heated in a temperature-controlled reservoir. Unlike either paraffin-wax or beeswax, this resin-based resist does not melt into a liquid. Instead, it becomes sticky, like treacle.

Next, a matching pair of engraved copper rollers applies the same pattern of gooey resist to both surfaces of the fabric simultaneously. As the coated fabric emerges from the rollers, a spray of cold water cools and hardens the resin. At this point, the resin appears dark brown against the white background of the undyed cotton fabric.

Then the cloth is dyed in the first colour, traditionally indigo. Because of the nature of indigo, this process is far from simple.

Merely dipping a fabric into indigo will not turn the fabric blue. To do its work, indigo needs oxygen. The indigo-dyed fabric must be removed from the vat and exposed to the air. As the indigo oxidises, the fabric turns from yellow to green to blue. Repeated indigo dips intensify and deepen the blue.

Wooden block used for overprinting supplementary colours

If you are hand-dyeing with indigo, you simply remove your fabric from the vat and hang it on a line in the fresh air. In the industrial setting of a wax print works, when you are dyeing thousands of metres at a time, you need a machine.

This turns out to be a complex construction of rollers, pulleys and overhead battens that carry the resist-coated fabric through a succession of indigo vats. Between each vat both surfaces of the fabric are exposed to the air and, hey presto, we have oxidation. The areas of the fabric that are not coated with resist turn blue.

Now for the first of our accidents, our first perfect imperfection.

The cooled resin resist that coats the fabric is now hard, like wax. As the fabric is moved and handled by the machinery, the resist suffers a spider web of minute cracks. Dye seeps through these cracks, resulting in the unique crackle effect we associate with wax print fabric.

When this new design feature proved very popular in Africa, the manufacturers had a problem. Because the cracks in the resist were purely accidental, the patterns they produced were random. This frustrated the manufacturers, who wanted to control the patterns completely.

Eventually, they began crumpling the fabric, before drawing it through an eye about six inches in diameter. This produced cracks along the length of the fabric, parallel to the selvedge, so at least they now had some measure of control.

For most wax prints, after the indigo dip, additional colours are then overprinted by machine using engraved rollers. This brings us to our second accident and the second perfect imperfection.

Historically, it was almost impossible to get a perfect alignment of pattern with each successive overprint of colour. This very slight mismatch of pattern, coupled with the accidental crackle effect, means that every single metre of wax print fabric is totally unique.

However, to further complicate things, not all wax prints are overprinted by roller machine. Even today, after the initial indigo dip, some fabrics are overprinted by hand using carved wooden blocks. Occasionally you might also see a wax print embossed with a shiny gold-leaf effect, which is a separate process.

When wax isn't wax: African fancy print

Genuine wax print is a unique and special textile. With its production methods straight out of the Industrial Revolution, making it is complicated, time-consuming and expensive, especially when compared with other printed fabrics.

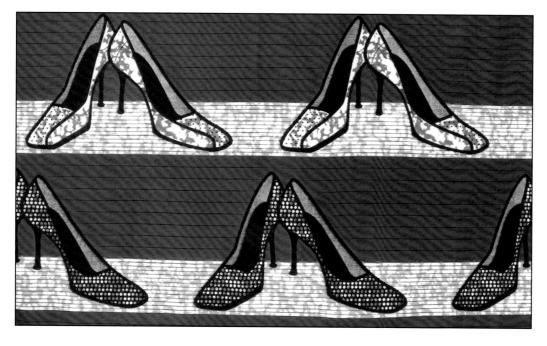

High Heels *design, fancy print*

However, it is possible to replicate wax print, without all the palaver and expense. In Africa, this category of fabric is called *fancy print*. It is a legitimate textile in its own right, with its own story to tell.

The technology to produce fancy print was developed in parallel with wax print technology, mainly as an easier and cheaper alternative. The fancy print we identify most with Africa is sometimes referred to as *imiwax* because that is just what it does: it imitates wax print.

To the untrained eye, this *imiwax* fancy print looks pretty much like wax print: the same bold colours, designs and inspiration; and often even the same crackle effect. But it differs in one important respect: unlike wax print, the design is printed on one side of the fabric only.

The first fancy prints were made using engraved metal rollers. Today, the technology has evolved to a rotary screen-printing process.

In the markets of West Africa, many of the fabrics on sale and worn by sellers and buyers alike are not genuine wax prints. They are fancy prints. Some are designed and produced in Africa for the African market; others are imported, both legally and illegally, from China.

Whatever their origin, because they are cheaper, fancy prints do have a legitimate place in the market. Very few Africans can afford wax prints imported from Europe. More can afford locally produced prints like those from ATL, GTP and, since 2006, Ghanaian ABC. But almost everyone can afford fancy prints.

Many fancy print designs mimic or even copy existing wax print designs. Also, because they are cheaper to produce, the manufacturers can take greater risks and experiment with new designs. The results are often wild, never boring and sometimes very, very funny.

Fancy print through history

From a technical and historical point of view, we can divide fancy print into six categories:

Imiwax imitates real wax in both design and colour. Whether from England, Holland, Africa or China, these prints are made to look genuinely African and sometimes it is difficult to distinguish them from the real thing.

Classic fancy prints, many with small flower motifs, do not generally look African. Historically, most of these fabrics were printed in Europe for export worldwide, including to Africa.

Fashion fancy prints are a modern development. Used mostly for clothing, these prints are a contemporary take on traditional African motifs. Many are designed and printed in Africa.

Speciality fancy prints are made for specific occasions where many people want to wear the same cloth, for example wedding or funeral cloths.

Commemorative or *political* prints are commissioned to mark special events.

Almost anything is fair game for reproduction on an African fancy print. In fact, some of these wild and wacky designs have even been made as wax prints as well.

A bright blue fabric adorned with lime green transistor radios ... why not?

A high-heeled shoe motif in bright blue and canary yellow ... surely a bestseller?

A needle and thread design ... perfect for the sewers and stitchers!

Livestock, birds and bicycles. Cars, electric fans and umbrellas. Computers, mobile phones and the Mercedes Benz logo.

Winston Churchill in full naval regalia with a Spitfire flying overhead.

Her Majesty Queen Elizabeth II, even.

Commemorative print: Africa's perfect canvas

'Churchill and The Queen,' you gasp. 'Emblazoned on an African fabric?'

'Why not?' we confirm. From the 1960s to the 1980s Nigerians couldn't get enough of these two defining icons of British-ness. A Queen Elizabeth design alone sold at least a million yards and the Calico Printers' Association (CPA) had to move production to its Zaire factory due to lack of capacity in England. And that wasn't any cheap fancy print that Nigerians clamoured for: it was genuine wax print.

This brings us to another aspect of modern Africa's fascination with printed textiles – *commemorative prints*, which often bear photographs, significant dates and social or political messages. In many ways, commemorative prints are a natural extension of the way Africans have used fabric throughout history.

Textiles have always played an important role in African societies. They are powerful markers, indicating wealth, power and status; and there is a long tradition of creating special cloths for special occasions.

For example, among the Kuba people of the Congo, when a new monarch ascends the throne a new Kuba cloth is commissioned to celebrate the event. In Ghana in 1923, when Prempeh I returned from exile as *asantahene* (ruler) of the ancient Ashante kingdom, a new Kente cloth was commissioned to mark the event. And for centuries the Yoruba of Nigeria have honoured important people with their distinctive resist-designed indigo cloths called Adire.

However, the designs on all of these traditional commemorative cloths are purely graphical. Their power comes from shape, colour and symbol, not from a depiction of the human form.

In the early 20th century this changed. Adire artists started using stencils cut from the metal lining of tea chests to apply a starch

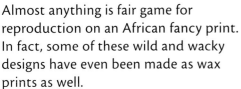

Post-independence Africa: commemorative designs evolve into political propaganda

resist to their cloths. Renditions of royal figures emerged, culminating in the 1935 Silver Jubilee cloth depicting the heads of King George V and Queen Mary. Eventually, Manchester's textile barons spotted a ready market and began exporting a printed cotton version to Nigeria, where it remained popular for years.

Producing a commemorative design as a wax print is certainly possible. In the ABC archive in Manchester the roll call of wax print celebrities includes Hisseine Habre of Chad, David Dacko of the Central African Republic, John F Kennedy and Queen Elizabeth II – all produced as complicated, expensive wax prints. The easier and cheaper alternative, of course, was fancy print. As we've seen, fancy print technology has always been available, alongside wax print.

By the 1960s, new presidents were emerging in post-colonial Africa. They needed a cheap publicity medium that would reach

the masses. It had to be colourful and easy to understand in largely illiterate countries. And, just in case the president was deposed before he'd paid his advertising bill, it had to be cheap. Fancy print fabric provided the perfect canvas.

Across the continent, ordinary citizens celebrated independence and a promising future. What better way to display national pride and honour your newly installed president than to wear a cloth bearing his smiling face and inauguration date? Significantly, the use and popularity of commemorative print is not limited to the political sphere. Far from it.

In addition to elections and revolutions, commemorative prints have celebrated all sorts of events: births and deaths; birthdays and anniversaries; pop concerts and sporting events; and presidential, royal and papal visits. Cloths have been

From the Congo to London: the medium is the message

I am a child of the '60s. I grew up in a world that the philosopher Marshall McLuan called 'the global village'. My T-shirts championed Ché, Marilyn and The Beatles. As McLuan said, 'the medium' really was 'the message'.

Flash forward to 1991. I'm sardined into a heaving, lurching London Underground carriage. I've spent the previous six years criss-crossing the deserts and forests of Africa. Just now, I'm on my way to work in my new career with a specialist African travel company.

It's Saturday morning, so I'm dressed casually in jeans and a shirt made of African fabric. This shirt is bright green, like the forests of the country it came from. It bears the slogan L'homme d'avenir. Le fondateur du M.P.R. 20 ans de la révolution, *and the disconcertingly beneficent image of a young Congolese man.*

Picture this man. I'm sure you can. He wears black horn-rimmed glasses and his trademark leopard-skin cap. He is Marshal Mobutu Sésé Seko Nkuku Ngbendu wa Za Banga. His name translates as The all-powerful warrior who, because of his endurance and inflexible will to win, will go from conquest to conquest, leaving fire in his wake *and he was once the President of Zaire (now the Democratic Republic of the Congo).*

Even then, the world knew and tolerated him as a despot and a tyrant. He was certainly that to the Congolese, who fled by the thousands to escape his regime of incompetence, corruption and cruelty.

Two such refugees, wearing dresses of brightly coloured and patterned African wax print fabric, sit across from me in the crush. Are they waitresses? Shop assistants? Cleaners? I doubt they are solicitors or bankers.

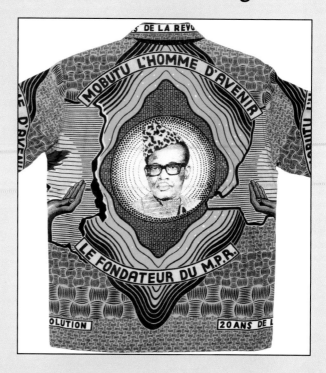

They stare at me, but they don't see me. All they see is the image on my shirt: Mobutu, the man who almost single-handedly ruined their immensely rich and completely impoverished country. They see the reason they are riding an Underground train to a badly paid job in a cold and foreign land, instead of raising their children in the bosom of their village compound.

If they said anything, I don't remember and it was probably in Lingala or French.

All I remember is how I felt. I never wore that shirt again.

Robert Irwin

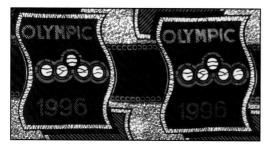

commissioned and printed for chiefs and dignitaries, governments and NGOs, schools and colleges, companies and trade unions, missions and churches.

In 2007, the British Museum collaborated with the University of Ghana to explore the role of commemorative prints in African society with 'Fabric of a Nation', an exhibition illustrating Ghana's first half-century of independence through a collection of wax and commemorative prints. The exhibition opened simultaneously in London and Accra, before touring the UK.

In 2010, the Tropenmuseum in Amsterdam mounted a major exhibition of African portrait cloths – 'Long Live the President'. The exhibition included cloths from the extensive private collections of Wolfgang Bender (Germany) and Bernard Collet (France).

Wax print celebrates the Olympics (left)

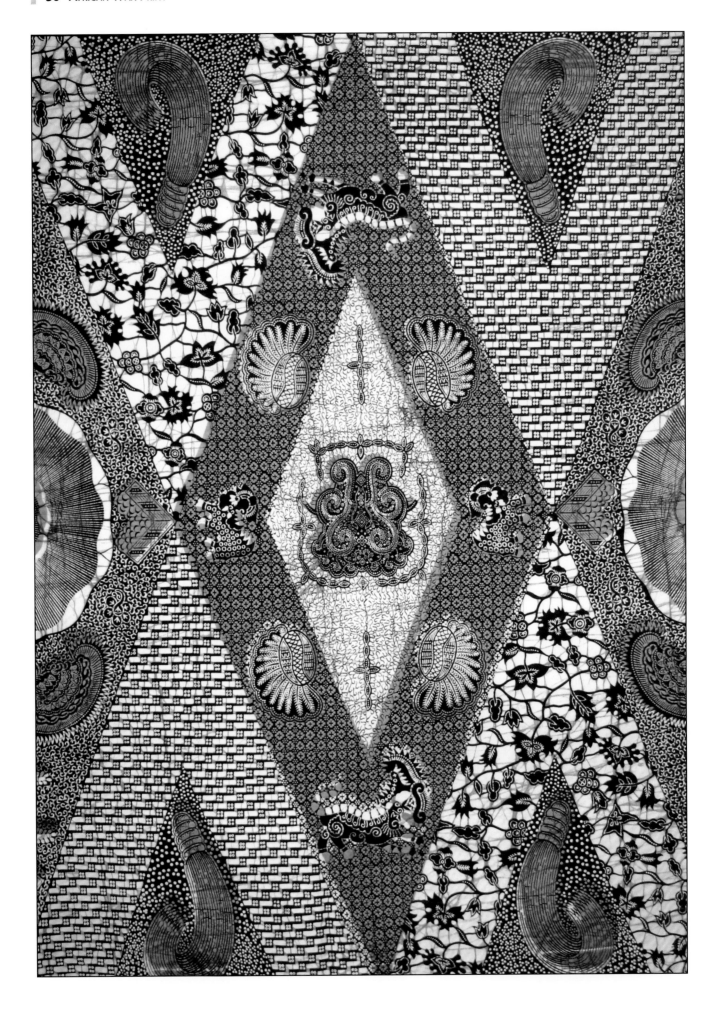

3 Wax print design

I am African

Wax print fabric, perhaps more than any of Africa's diverse textile traditions, is a defining metaphor of African design, fashion and expression. Across most of Africa and around the world, wax print is an instantly identifiable signal.

Wherever we see it, wax print shouts at us – loudly, proudly and without compromise: 'This is African.' And more importantly: 'I am African.'

Plain and simple, wax print fabric just *looks* African.

So, what makes these designs so African? Where did they come from and how have they evolved since Ebenezer Brown Fleming's first speculative shipment landed in the Gold Coast over 100 years ago?

Design evolution: Java, Europe and Africa

Wax print as a concept was inspired by Java batik, so it follows that the first designs exported from England and Holland to Africa mimicked Javanese/Indonesian designs. Butterflies, scorpions, fish and trailing leaves are early examples of this design influence (or perhaps even its thievery).

Today, we recognise the sacred Garuda bird as a symbol of Indonesia. A design based on the head and tail feathers of the Garuda has appeared in various forms as a wax print. Interestingly, in Africa designs inspired by the Garuda have had several different names: in Ghana – *Bunch of Bananas*; in Burkina Faso – *The Mask*; in Côte d'Ivoire – *Shell*; and in Togo – *Snail Out of His Shell*.

Clearly, even dating back to the earliest wax prints, the African perception and interpretation of design varies from region to region. The head of ABC's design studio described another example in a trade press article, *circa* 1960. A new ABC wax print hit the market in Nigeria on the same day that government workers received a pay rise. ABC's name for the fabric became instantly irrelevant and to this day in Nigeria it is still called *The Bonus*.

Egyptian motifs – mummies, pyramids and the ankh symbol – also crept into some early wax print designs, but these fell from favour in the early 20th century.

Indonesian Sawat *design batik (left) and wax print: both inspired by the Garuda*

A bunch of bananas, a shell or a mask? It all depends where you live

Over time, as wax print became more and more popular in West Africa, the European producers adapted to local taste and included more African symbolism in their designs.

The related concepts of kingship and authority have inspired many wax designs. Around 1904 the English and Dutch both launched a design, still popular today, called the *Sword of Kingship* (also called *Staff of Kingship*). It is based on the *akofena* or royal sword of the *Asantehene*, ruler of the Ashanti kingdom in central Ghana.

The Sword of Kingship (below and opposite top): classic designs are updated year after year

The same design exists in Nigeria, Côte d'Ivoire and Mali, except the name has been localised to *The Corkscrew*, while in Togo it is called *The Axe*. Similarly, *The Royal Stool*, another powerful Ashanti symbol, is known in Togo as *The Stool of Unmarried Women*.

Education is a highly valued commodity in Africa. Not surprisingly, it has been a prominent theme in wax print design. The popular *Alphabet* pattern has gone through multiple variations over the years, from simple representations of children's blocks and letters on a chalkboard to computer motifs. Since hitting the market in the 1920s, these *Alphabet* designs have proudly trumpeted the status of the wearer: 'I am educated and I am literate.'

Education often crops up in conjunction with other more traditional African themes. A pattern called *Hand and Fingers* shows the upturned palm of a hand surrounded by rows of detached fingers, with the hand holding twelve pennies. This design is very old (one source says 1895, another 1905) and has been available in various forms from several companies ever since. ABC alone has printed it in up to 30 different colourways.

The education theme is expressed by the twelve pennies, which make up one shilling. In Africa, or for that matter anywhere, what could be more educational than how to add up your pennies?

Digging deeper into the *Hand and Fingers* design, we find another universal theme: interdependence. This theme works on multiple levels, from the nation and tribe all the way down to the village, the compound and the family. Just as the hand is useless without the fingers, the ruler or village elder cannot function without the support of the people.

In Islamic countries, the hand represents the *Hand of Fatima*, symbolising the five obligations of Islam – faith, prayer, fasting, charity and pilgrimage. It is also a powerful talisman against the evil eye.

For Africans, the sanctity of the family is extremely important. Parents are devoted to their children, children respect their parents

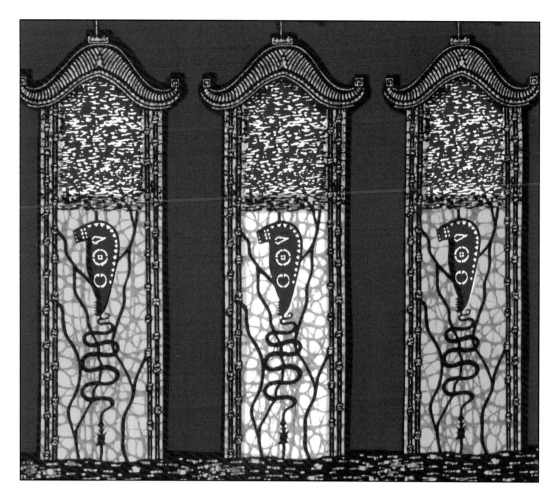

The Alphabet *design shows respect for education*

and everybody honours their ancestors. The related themes of family and fertility figure prominently in wax print design.

To induce fertility, a woman may wear a design called *Tree of Life*. Then, if she successfully conceives, her husband may present her with a print called *The Good Husband*. (Why this design isn't called *The Good Wife*, we leave to speculation!)

Of course, not every design comes complete with a provenance of symbolic meaning. In other cases, the original meaning may have been lost. *New Fine Trail* is an intricate pattern of interlaced stems, leaves and flowers; *Dice* is a checkerboard of tiny die faces showing four spots. Over the years, each of these designs has been printed in many colourways and in huge volumes, but so far we have not uncovered their origin or meaning. But we will keep looking.

Another major wax print theme (which also spills over into cheaper fancy print technology) is the commemorative or anniversary print. Usually incorporating a portrait of a president, chief or other dignitary, these designs were, and still are, commissioned to celebrate special events, such as coronations, inaugurations and even revolutions. We looked at this phenomenon in more detail in Chapter 2.

Hand and Fingers *design (right) worn in Bandiagara market, Mali; classic* New Fine Trail *in indigo by GTP, Ghana*

Design authenticity: is it *really* African?

What do we know about the talented graphic artists who create the wax print designs that we now label as quintessentially African?

The most significant and surprising thing is: they are *not* African. When they shut down their computers and leave their studios, these artists are not in Lagos or Lomé or Accra. They are in Hyde in Greater Manchester, or Helmond in The Netherlands. Historically, that is the way it's always been, Europeans designing for Africa. (Today, some design work is done in Africa, but the majority is still in Europe.)

Despite not actually being African, wax print designers really do know the African market and mindset. By studying the design archives, they understand and appreciate the wax print traditions. Plus, by travelling regularly to Africa and interacting with their customers, they stay tuned-in to current African tastes and trends. They know what's hot and what's not. And, to some degree, their creativity helps determine African opinion and drive African fashion.

Looking back for inspiration: 2009 design (left) and possible 1990s source of inspiration

So are their designs, created in Europe for Africa, really *African*? Were they ever? And what are the connections between traditional, indigenous African design and wax print?

Afro-European or Euro-African? Pioneering market research

As we've seen, the earliest wax designs were Javanese, followed quickly by more 'African' adaptations as the English and Dutch tried to capture the imaginations and the money of their African buyers.

So was the European relationship with the African market *reactive* or *proactive*?

Did the European companies copy existing African designs, assuming that because they were already popular, they would sell? Or did they create their own, speculative designs, and just hope that they took off?

Actually, it was a bit of both. In the process, and maybe even without realising it, the wax print industry pioneered the modern notion of market research.

Looking back to the early days of English wax print, research suggests that the designers may not have been particularly important. They may have worked less on their own initiative and more on detailed instructions, either from the manufacturers or from the merchant firms that commissioned the fabrics in the first place.

Whether a new wax design sold (or not) depended on many factors: culture, language, religion, and so on. And, because the merchants had the most to gain (or to lose), they took a keen interest in reading the market and making sure that their designs were just right.

As the market developed and the profits rolled in, the merchants and their agents on the ground in Africa started to appreciate some kind of *African aesthetic*, with its rich cultural diversity and inherent sense of style. Eventually, those perceptions fed into the instructions the merchants gave the manufacturers and the manufacturers gave their designers.

Some of these instructions survive in the archives, in the sample tabs and order books that document the transactions between the manufacturers and their merchant customers.

Around the turn of the 20th century, Manchester wax print merchant Charles Beving made detailed written suggestions about tailoring designs for the African taste. Beving, like other merchants and manufacturers of the era, built an extensive collection of Javanese and traditional African textiles, which were adapted as design sources for wax print. (See the panel on page 42.)

A revealing piece of the puzzle: The Beving Collection

The scraps of information that tell the story of African wax print fabric remain scattered and elusive, literally a bolt here and a swatch there.

Thanks to the generosity of one Manchester textile family, one very important piece of the puzzle remains intact: The Beving Collection.

The collection was compiled by its namesake, Charles Beving, founder of the Manchester textile company Blakely & Beving, later Beving & Co.

Begun in the 1880s, Beving's collection of 200 West African textiles, 100 Javanese cloths, plus some other related items, was first displayed in 1933 when Beving's son gave it to the Manchester City Art Gallery. Today it is housed and curated by the British Museum.

One very interesting and illuminating aspect of the collection is the commentary, much of it written by Charles Beving himself, that is attached to many of the fabrics.

Here, Beving remarks in detail on a fabric's design:

The general effect of this sarong with its sort of 10,000 character ground would lead me to think at first that it ought to do for Japan. But one thing … is the lotus flowers and leaf which is [sic] only seen and used in Buddhist funerals in Japan and otherwise used means bad luck. If these can be eliminated and another flower substituted to accord with the rest of the design it would do well.

What was Beving driving at?

Well, as a textile baron trading into West Africa, he may have been viewing this particular fabric as a design source.

Beving seems to be saying, 'Change the lotus, which means *bad luck*, to another flower, and the design might be successful in the African market' – in effect, an early form of market research.

Yongolo *wax print, 1990: CPA label (opposte left), art work (centre) and multiple colourways (right)*

The Brunnschweiler archive contains similar snippets of evidence. A sample of indigo-dyed cloth has a note attached, asking for the design to be made 'a little more busy'. Someone has drawn a revised, busier design in pencil directly onto the fabric. Another indigo fabric, possibly from a competitor, has a memo attached. Dated 1901, it's from a merchant asking the Newton Bank print works to copy the darker blue of the sample.

From clues like this, we see the early interaction between manufacturers and designers in Europe and their African customers. At ABC, this relationship continues to this day. Tasked with creating new designs for the sophisticated and demanding African market, where can the 21st-century designers turn for inspiration?

In addition to the various books, articles, dissertations and other source materials that document African textile and artistic heritage, there are extensive company archives: ABC alone has some 35,000 designs on record, either as finished fabrics or as original, hand-drawn designs.

At the same time, information pours in constantly from Africa about patterns and colourways that are already selling. How can these be combined and adapted to create new, even more successful designs? The possibilities are virtually limitless … well, not quite.

As we've seen, compared with modern fabric printing, wax print is relatively complicated. The process itself (applying the resist, plus overprinting either by roller or hand-blocking) places certain technical restrictions on the designers. Some ideas, however good they are, just can't be made as wax prints. Fortunately, these designs may still find their way to market as fancy prints.

The colours of Africa

Colour and wax print are inseparable. Even when a design comes to market in a simple indigo-on-white colourway, there is something about the colour that radiates like no other blue.

Do wax prints in general, or specific wax designs, favour particular colours? Are certain colour combinations taboo?

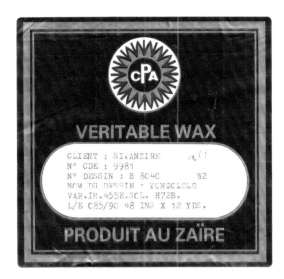

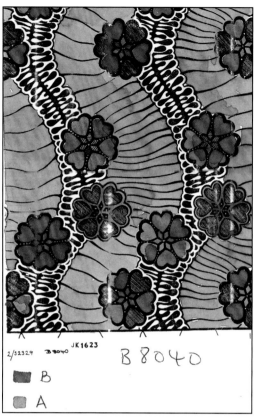

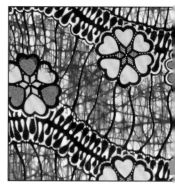

With so many thousands of designs and colourways on the market and in the archives, it's almost impossible to tell.

Sometimes you see a colourway and think, 'What a surprising combination!' It just works. At other times you wonder, 'Who had that crazy idea?' Either way, it hardly matters. Somewhere in Africa somebody is looking at the same fabric and thinking, 'Wow! I want it.'

As for the colourways themselves, certain colour combinations seem to be perennially popular: claret and blue; red and yellow; green and orange; and indigo. Also, the popularity of colours varies from country to country and in large, diverse countries like Nigeria, from region to region.

In any event, when a fabric proves popular and profitable, the manufacturers often reprint the design in new colourways. It's amazing how different the same design can look, just by changing its colours.

England v Holland: the copyright conundrum

Enter a fabric kiosk or stroll through a market almost anywhere in Africa, and you'll see a mind-boggling array of wax print designs. Some will be new, this season's latest offerings, hot off the rollers. Others will be older designs, perhaps in production since the early 20th century.

'How many designs are there?' you wonder. Quite honestly, it's impossible to say.

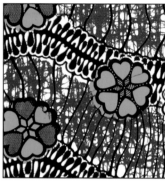

For many of the oldest wax print designs, who exactly owns what remains controversial, with both English and Dutch producers laying claims.

While the precise origins of these contentious designs remain shrouded in the mists of time, one name keeps popping up in the story – none other than Ebenezer Brown Fleming.

Brown Fleming, acting as sole agent for the Haarlem Cotton Company (HKM), was responsible for marketing that company's fabric in West Africa. The records are unclear and incomplete, but research suggests that Brown Fleming may have been more than just a salesman. He may have played a more proactive role, feeding information about designs back from the African market to his Dutch client.

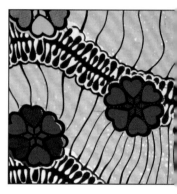

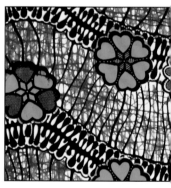

Meanwhile, around 1900, Brown Fleming registered some of the Haarlem designs under his own name in England. HKM closed down in 1917 and sold its printing rollers to another Dutch producer, PF van Vlissingen (now Vlisco). Quite reasonably, van Vlissingen assumed that its investment included copyright to the designs.

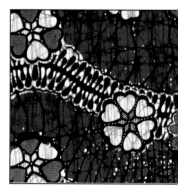

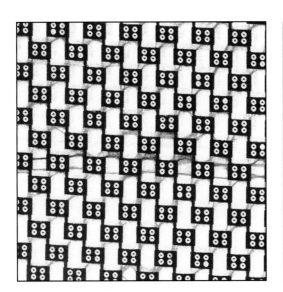

Dice – 25 million yards and still going strong; and an unknown design – all but forgotten

Brown Fleming's company continued trading after his death in 1912, but was taken over in 1939 by the Calico Printers Association of Manchester. Quite reasonably – haven't we heard this before? – the CPA assumed that their investment included copyright to the designs. Decades and numerous discussions later, we still only know one thing for sure: for many designs, nobody can prove 100% incontestable ownership.

Whoops! – when designs fail

Imagine for a moment that you are a wax print manufacturer. Your aim, pure and simple, is to design and print fabrics that will sell in sufficient volumes to make money.

Consider the variables that stand in your way. Your fabric's design, colourway and meaning must all work together to capture the imagination and fancy of your target market, the ladies of West Africa.

Also, you can't cut corners on quality. Your cotton, dyes and printing must meet the high standards demanded by your discerning buyers. One historical account from France published in 1954 describes African women tasting fabrics for saltiness as a test of dye-fastness and fabric quality.

It's a tall order, with many variables and a high potential for very expensive errors.

Now, compare the wax print business with something less risky: making buckets, say. All you need is a bucket that holds water and doesn't leak, at an affordable price.

If you want to get really fancy, you can offer different colours. But compared with wax print, the bucket business is pretty simple.

So, given the comparative complexity of the wax print business, is it any wonder that some designs arrive with great fanfare in the markets of West Africa, only to be ignored and even shunned by potential buyers? The myriad examples, whether amusing or serious, are usually culturally significant.

What about a nice owl pattern? From the European point of view, it was an appealing design with a great sense of fun, a potential bestseller. But what the designers didn't know is this: in parts of West Africa, when an owl settles on your roof it means someone in your house is going to die. Whoops! Somewhere, maybe in Africa, maybe in a warehouse in Europe, there's an awful lot of cute owl fabric still waiting for a buyer.

How about a striking, intricate maze of colourful lines and figures? When this fabric hit the market in Nigeria it initially did very well. Until, that is, an Islamic cleric examined it and saw actual words written in Arabic script. He forbade anyone from sitting on the words, which made the fabric useless as a wrap-around. Overnight, the fabric was dead in the market.

Another more solemn example concerns a classic design called *Skin*. From a distance, it appears to be a graphical interpretation of snakeskin. However, the devil is in the detail. If you move closer and examine the tiny patterning on the scales of the snakeskin,

A little fabric shop in Manchester

Imagine yourself back in another place and another time: Manchester in 1960. You are shopping. Naturally, because you have a passion for creating and for textiles, fabric permanently tops your mental shopping list.

It is cold and grey and raining, probably sideways. You stumble upon a fabric shop. It is small and cosy and very different from any fabric shop you have ever been in. Its shelves are packed with exotic, brightly coloured prints, fabrics you have only seen until now in the pages of a *National Geographic* magazine.

These are genuine wax print fabrics, the same fabrics you might find in Makola market in Accra or Balogun market in Lagos. You are surprised and fascinated, not just by the vibrant colours and bold designs, but also the quality of this fabric – beautifully woven cotton with a gorgeous feel.

'Where,' you wonder, 'could these wonderful fabrics come from?'

'From here, from Manchester,' answers Len Walker, the manager. 'This is A Brunnschweiler & Co.'s retail outlet. Most of our fabric is exported to Africa, but a small amount is sold here, in England.'

Now another customer, smartly dressed, enters the tiny shop. Mr Walker greets him at length with warmth and respect. Then, he begins pulling 12 yard lengths of fabric from the shelves for his customer to admire and assess.

You watch and listen. The man's English bears an accent that isn't Mancunian and his pockets are deep. He buys many pieces and because it is a time before credit cards he pays cash – lots of cash.

After he leaves, Mr Walker returns to you.

'Chief Iffie,' he explains. 'From Lagos. He comes here often. So does Chief Etchi of Warri. And Chief Otite, but he doesn't come as far. He lives in London.'

Inspired and loosely based on an account found in an undated, unidentified magazine; probably a trade journal published *circa* 1960.

Skin, *ABC wax print*

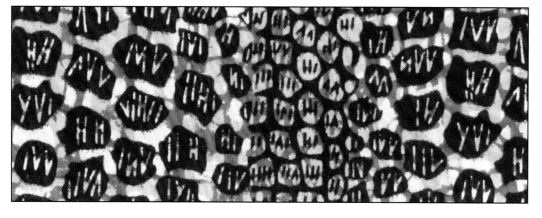

you *might* think you see three letters – VIH. Not a problem in countries like Ghana and Nigeria, but in French West Africa we have *un grand problème* indeed: VIH is the three-letter acronym for *Virus de l'Immunodéficience Humaine* (in English, HIV).

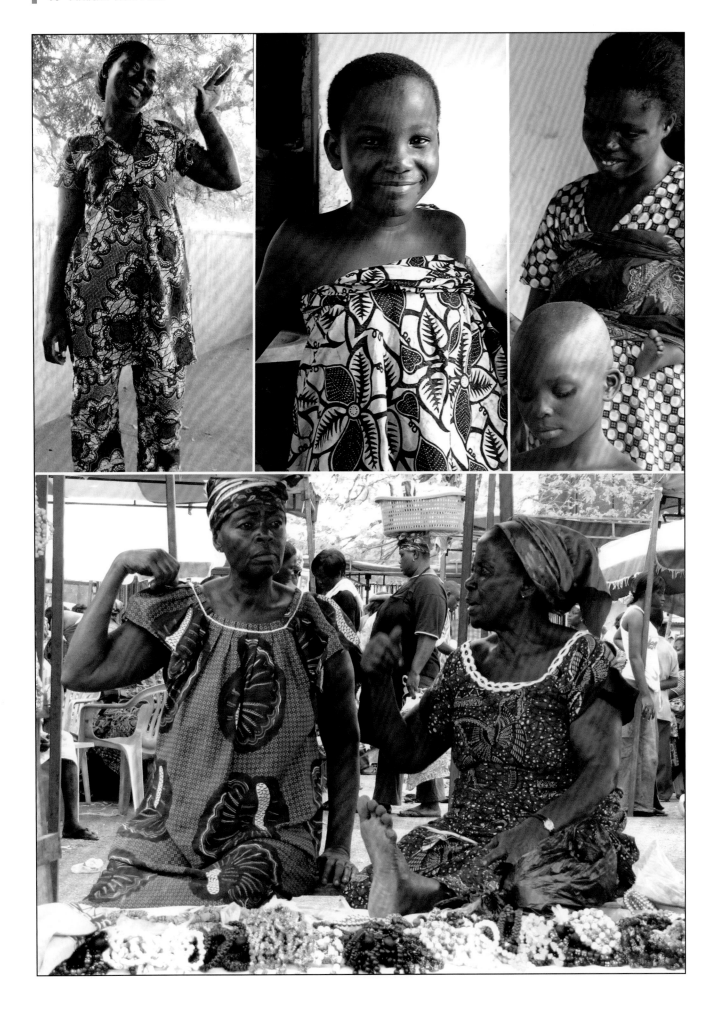

4 Wax print in Africa

You are what you wear

Africa is a continent of contrasts. In remote villages, women and children still walk miles to fetch their daily water and firewood. Yet in these same villages, the tallest structure is no longer the mosque or church steeple: it's the mobile phone mast.

Regardless of where you go in Africa, from the humblest village compound to the most ostentatious mansions of Lagos or Nairobi, Africans exude one ever present constant: *style*. From Accra to Abidjan and Zambia to Zanzibar, it doesn't matter how much money you have or where you live on the status ladder – 'you are what you wear'.

All over Africa, wax print is worn every day by men, women and children, either as tailored clothing or as simple *pagnes* or wrappers. Wax print is in the market, in schools, in offices, on the street. Quite literally, it's everywhere.

Child carrying a doll, Ghana (top); fetching wood, Congo (left); Manjima Jatta, fabric vendor, The Gambia (right)

The *pagne*: everyday or formal wear

In the West, everyday dress has become extremely casual. Jeans and T-shirts are almost formal compared with shell suits, and mothers have been spotted wearing pyjamas on the school run. An African

Across West Africa: Wherever you look – wax print

woman would be shocked. Even if she is just going to the market for rice, she will dress respectably in the best she can afford. So will her husband and children.

Most African women cannot afford to wear wax print every day. But depending on personal means, there is an exception: the ubiquitous *pagne*. This 2 yard length of fabric is simply tied around the waist so that it covers the legs from hip to ankle. For everyday wear, it usually complements a Western blouse or T-shirt. The *pagne* is comfortable, functional and always in fashion. For many women, wax print may be displaced by the cheaper fancy print as the fabric of necessity. In either case, even though the *pagne* may be old and well worn, it will always be meticulously laundered.

The *pagne* can also be part of a more formal ensemble, especially in francophone Africa, where elegance is almost a vocation. On top, there are three options: a long, loose-fitting over-garment called a *ndoket*; a loose, hip-length blouse with wide sleeves called a *marinière*; or a tighter-fitting blouse with a low neck, hip flounce and wide sleeves called a *taille basse*. A matching head-tie, of course, is the finishing touch.

So do all Africans dress *African*? No – Western styles, brands and logos play a big role in African fashion. At the same time, traditional costumes and fabrics – including wax print – remain mainstream and popular. There are several reasons for this. Wax print is expressive – it tells a story. It is identified with Africa, despite its Indonesian and European roots. And it is aspirational: people start out buying fancy print and graduate to wax print when they can afford it.

Wax print *couture*

Now transport yourself to Africa and imagine: you want a new outfit. Correction – you *need* a new outfit! The occasion is important, maybe a wedding or anniversary, a christening or a traditional naming ceremony. You need something that speaks – no, *shouts* – 'Look at me. Admire my status, achievement and good taste.'

You consider your budget and weigh your options. A high street emporium in the market and a frock off the peg? Affordable,

but boring. The *mitumba* market for a second-hand designer garment, mined from the tons of charity clothing that arrive by the container-load from Europe and America? Fashionable, but so 'not African'.

No, this is an important occasion. You must show your respect and you must be respected. You have no other choice. You must spend big on a tailor-made outfit of meticulously selected wax print. 'Besides, wax print lasts. I can wear it for years,' you rationalise.

And so, to the market and a little stall you know. This lady always has wax print in an

excellent variety of colours, patterns and quality, including prestige *marques* like ABC and Vlisco. She only stocks 12 yard pieces as they come from the factory – the standard selling length. Sometimes she will cut to supply 6 yards, but only at a price.

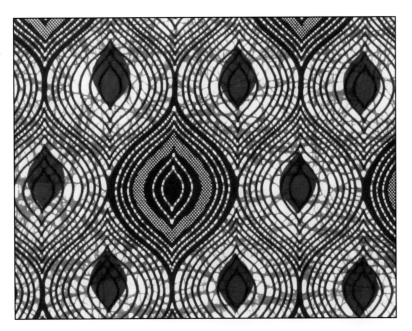

Wax print speaks: either by design – Onion Chips or Eye of My Rival (above) – or by logo

of wax print left over. You'll take that too and toss it casually over your shoulder. What better way to say, 'I can afford it.'

Logo worship: it's all on the selvedge

Today, in our global village, brand recognition is universal. In other words, logos count, even in Africa. Street boys selling phone cards sport the Nike tick and taxi-drivers wear Rolex. In this logo-fixated world, is it any wonder that African women are so instantly aware of the selvedge on their wax print fabrics?

Regardless of your status or your budget, your selvedge says it all, with messages like: *Real English Wax, Véritable Wax Anglais, Real Dutch Wax, Véritable Wax Hollandais, Guaranteed Wax Printed in Ghana* or *Guaranteed Real Wax Hitarget.*

As with any fashion statement, your selvedge must of course be visible to the world. When you have a dress made in Africa, you don't cut off the selvedge. You make sure it is placed prominently in the design for all to see and admire. Even if you are only wearing your cloth as a simple wrapper, you turn it right side out so that the selvedge is legible.

To your difficult choice of colour and design, add another factor. You are your husband's first wife and your fabric will speak directly to his second wife. Your relationship is amicable, with an undertone of jealousy. Aha! What's this? A subtle, dignified print in brown and red. Perfect. The design represents eyes that are red with tears. Its official name is *Onion Chips*, but its alternative name is more appropriate: *Eye of My Rival*.

Now, to the garment itself. You'll need three pieces, of course: skirt, blouse and head-tie. Your fabric vendor's house tailor is fine for everyday wear, but you have someone special in mind for this creation. Her catalogue of patterns is extensive and she always adds a creative twist that makes her outfits unique. Sometimes, she's even able to integrate the pattern of the fabric, *à la décollage*, into the design and cut of the garment – now that *is* clever.

After a specialist embroiderer adds the finishing touches, your outfit will be ready for the discerning and critical eyes of your family, friends and rival. And oh, look: there's a length

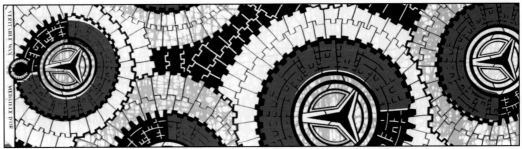

So does the selvedge ever lie? In truth, sometimes it does. Counterfeit Chinese wax prints and poor-quality fancy prints may both be labelled as *Véritable Real Wax* (right). Can you spot the difference?

In the helter-skelter of the market, unless you know your fabrics, it really is a case of 'buyer beware'.

The fabric market: *Bon soir,* Nana Benz

Around the world, one luxury brand stands above all others as the logo of success – Mercedes-Benz. In Africa, a Mercedes – even an old one – is all you need to say, 'I've made it.' Even if you can't afford the car, you can aspire to it by wearing a logo-emblazoned wax print, or walling your compound with logo-inspired cement blocks.

In Africa's francophone countries, especially in Togo, this unmistakable *marque* of wealth has been adopted by the very successful and sometimes very rich class of women who wheel and deal at the pinnacle of the local fabric markets. The members of this elite tribe of savvy traders have a nickname: *Nana Benz.*

Look around Africa's markets and you're struck by a definite imbalance of the sexes: the majority of sellers, especially in the textile trade, are women. And there's one thing you can be certain about – these ladies are very good at business. Their goal is always the same: to separate you from your money. They need to feed their children and, with any luck, put a little aside to invest in their business. Some of them might not be able to read, but they can count zeros and speak several languages. They'll spot a customer at a hundred yards and they probably know exactly which piece of fabric you want before you do.

Magie Relph with fabric merchant Evelyn, Makola Market, Accra

Fabric vendor, Koforidua, Ghana

See that woman with a bowl of fabrics on her head, wandering like all the others through the dusty aisles of the market? She's selling *pagnes* – pieces of wax or fancy print cut into 2 yard lengths to be worn as wrappers. If she works hard, if she buys smart and sells well, in a few years she'll have a table and after that an official market stall. Then she'll be selling 12 yard lengths of fabric, both to the public and to the *pagne* sellers.

After more hard work and hustling, she'll move into a shop with a ceiling fan and a door that locks. She'll have rack upon rack of wax and fancy print fabrics, stacked to the rafters. She'll have nieces and neighbours as shop assistants. At the end of the day, after coining a healthy profit, she'll send a text on her mobile phone. Her Mercedes will pull up. Her driver will hold the door and greet her politely, '*Bon soir*, Nana Benz.'

Wax print as propaganda

As we have seen, in Africa wax print is more than mere fabric – it's a medium of expression. Although some wax designs utilise text, the majority rely on strong graphical symbolism to convey their message.

Given the overall low rate of literacy in Africa, can you think of a more powerful advertising or propaganda medium than the ever-popular, ubiquitous wax print? Is it any wonder that Africa's ambitious politicians have exploited established wax designs for political ends?

In Côte d'Ivoire, a candidate running for his party's presidential nomination adapted the popular *Alphabet* design to publicise his campaign. However, instead of using the letters ABC, he used RDA-PDCI, the acronym for his political party. His subtle but effective message was: 'Vote for me as president because I will be as reliable and long-lasting as the *Alphabet* design.' He won.

Another example, this one with a slightly less subtle message, is the *Six Spark Plugs* design (or in French – *Six Bougies*), which was introduced in the Belgian Congo in the 1940s and is still popular there today.

Technology marches on: wax print documents it all

The design shows six spark plugs radiating out from the face of an unnamed woman. The spark plugs come from a six-cylinder car, a symbol of strength and power. However, the imaginative Congolese saw something different – a woman encircled by an array of six phalluses.

Colour, chaos and hope: wax print as metaphor

It's a sensation I will never forget. I felt assaulted by the shouting, the smells and the blinding light. Behind me was the safety net of my British-ness: middle-class, suburban and very, very white. Sprawled before me was the colour and chaos of my first African market. I was shopping for vegetables, so I waded in.

In both time and experience, that was a long time ago: 1984 in the City Market off Lumumba Road, Lusaka. The copper market had crashed and Zambia was crippled. Shelves were bare, fuel was a luxury and rice was like gold. Women vendors sat on the ground with their wares. All they had to sell were small piles of onions and tomatoes.

Despite the heat, dust and depression of their poverty, to me, those vegetable ladies were a revelation and a wonder. Shouting, bargaining, gossiping, nursing and scolding their multitudes of children, somehow they seemed to float above their dire circumstances.

'Why is that?' I wondered. And then it hit me. 'It's what they're wearing. It's their fabrics.'

All around me black women wore bright, bold, patterned cloths, wrap-around style. Their babies were strapped to their backs with even more colourful fabrics. When they rose to walk – tin bowls of vegetables balanced on their heads – their backs were straight and their heads held high.

Their wrappers, of course, were what really grabbed me and I had to have one. I found the fabric stalls and struck a deal. Probably I paid too much, but who cares? I wore that fabric every day for weeks, as I travelled overland, north to Nairobi. It was my first piece of African fabric and I was hooked.

Looking back now, after more than twenty years of travel, research and experience, I wonder, 'Was it a genuine wax print?' I doubt it. In 1980s Zambia, wax print was expensive and correspondingly rare. It was probably an imiwax or fancy print, but that hardly matters.

What does matter is this: for a novice in Africa, Lusaka market was a jolting reminder of Africa's inequity and poverty. It was also my first lesson in the pride, resilience and hope that Africans rely on to survive. For me, the fabrics became a symbol of that very African spirit.

Magie Relph

Either interpretation is ripe for exploitation, and so it was. In the tumultuous 1960s, following the Congo's independence from Belgium, presidential hopeful Moïse Tshombe had a new version of *Six Spark Plugs* printed in Holland, replacing the woman with his own picture. He won, but didn't last long. He was quickly deposed by Mobutu, who over the next four decades commissioned millions of yards of wax and fancy print bearing his disconcertingly beneficent visage.

With many political prints worn simply as *pagnes*, how you wrap and wear your cloth tells the world in clear terms what you think about a politician. You could display an image of the president upside down. Or, by ensuring the president's picture is wrapped to the back, every time you sit down you will be making a strong and unmistakable political statement.

Mapping change: the people's newspaper

For historians and social anthropologists, wax print (and its sister fabric, *imiwax* or fancy print) provides a dynamic, evolving record of modern Africa's changing values, hopes and aspirations. Politics, society and relationships all get blanket coverage in the 'people's newspaper' – the fabrics that Africans use and wear every day.

Through commemorative prints we've seen the winds of change blow across the political landscape. In staunchly anti-apartheid Tanzania in the 1980s, we found a fabric bearing a political map of Africa surrounded by its national flags. It was an accurate map, but something was missing: South Africa did not exist. When Nelson Mandela was released from prison and the 'rainbow nation' was born, this print was re-issued and South Africa was at last included in the African family of nations.

Through the fabrics printed with images of everyday objects, we can see each new wave of Western consumer technology breaking on the shores of Africa, changing lives for better or for worse. The fabrics have

documented it all: bicycles became motor-bikes; transistor radios became MP3 players; conventional telephones became mobile cell phones. What do these changing fabric motifs tell us? What would an African say?

Well, an African woman – maybe selling dried fish or mobile phone cards, perhaps fetching firewood or pounding millet – might reply: 'I too live in the global village – and I too want a piece of the pie.' Who can blame her?

Pounding millet, Sukuta, The Gambia

Magie Relph *African Calliope*

I made my first quilt while working and travelling in Africa in the 1980s, inspired by the fabrics I collected in markets along the way. Despite the influence of African wax print on the design, the blocks are quite traditional. So was the method – hand piecing over paper – except that I used cardboard and a stapler. This quilt (220 x 205 cm) holds fond memories, as many of the fabrics were scraps donated by friends after they'd had clothes made by the local tailors.

5 Inspired by wax print

Magie Relph introduces the selected textile art

Fabric – especially African fabric – grabs me.

As a quilter and textile artist, African fabric has a way of taking hold of my imagination and pushing me to create. And wax print – I suppose because it was the fabric that really blew me away when I first ventured into the teeming turmoil of an African market – grabs me the most.

I'm not the only one.

In the world of fashion, wax print has periodically splashed onto the catwalks – most recently in the 2010 collections of Cristobal Balenciaga and Juanjo Olivia (for Gucci).

Wax print has also made significant appearances in contemporary art. Numerous adventurous artists – some famous, some less so – have explored and exploited its heritage, symbolism, colour and design.

Samuel Fosso, the Cameroon-born photographer based in the Central African Republic, became a reluctant celebrity in the 1990s with his self-portraits, often dressed up in wax print. Many of the giant canvases of American painter and portraitist Kehinde Wiley have featured wax print as a cultural foil to the classic poses of his models. British artist Grace Ndiritu has experimented with wax print in her video-portrait-installation art.

Perhaps the most well-known of all, however, is Yinka Shonibare, MBE. British-born, but raised in Lagos, Shonibare has almost made wax print his creative trade mark. For example, his *Three Graces* (2001) is a life-sized display of three Victorian ladies: they are headless and wear wax print.

'Why the wax print?' you wonder. Interviewed in conjunction with his 2004 nomination for the Turner Prize, he replied, 'They prove to have a crossbred cultural background quite of their own. And it's the fallacy of that signification that I like. It's the way I view culture – it's an artificial construct.'

That may be so. But I don't think there is anything 'artificial' about the textile art we have included here for you to think about and hopefully admire and enjoy. All of these wonderful pieces – mostly quilts, with a few items of art wear – were created by customers of our small fair trade business dealing in African textiles. Through their enthusiasm and love of the fabrics, we've now become friends.

Janice Gunner *African Odyssey I & African Odyssey V*

My inspiration as a quilter and stitched textile artist comes from the tactile nature of the cloth itself. I've never been to sub-Saharan Africa, but an introduction to African fabrics by Magie led to my 'African Odyssey' series of quilts. I feel particularly challenged and inspired by wax print: how can I use the bold designs and colours and integrate them into my own artistic style?

African Odyssey I,
132 x 102 cm

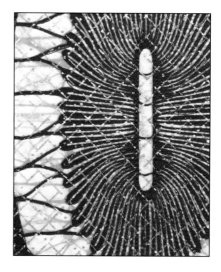

African Odyssey V, 115 x 37 cm

Jane Rowland *Safari Njema & Ushanga*

Africa means a lot to me. I grew up in Tanganyika, Uganda and Kenya; then, after teaching in Nairobi, I lived and travelled for thirteen years in Nigeria and Ghana. I still return to Africa whenever I can and its colours, designs, textures and traditions are a constant memory and influence.

Ushanga – 'beads' in Swahili – is a beaded curtain I made from recycled scraps of wax print, bark cloth, hessian, raffia, felt and paper. For me, it represents the ingenuity of Africans. *Safari Njema*, or 'good journey', is my first quilt using wax print, inspired by African strip weaving and the work of Yinka Shonibare.

Safari Njema,
240 x 230 cm

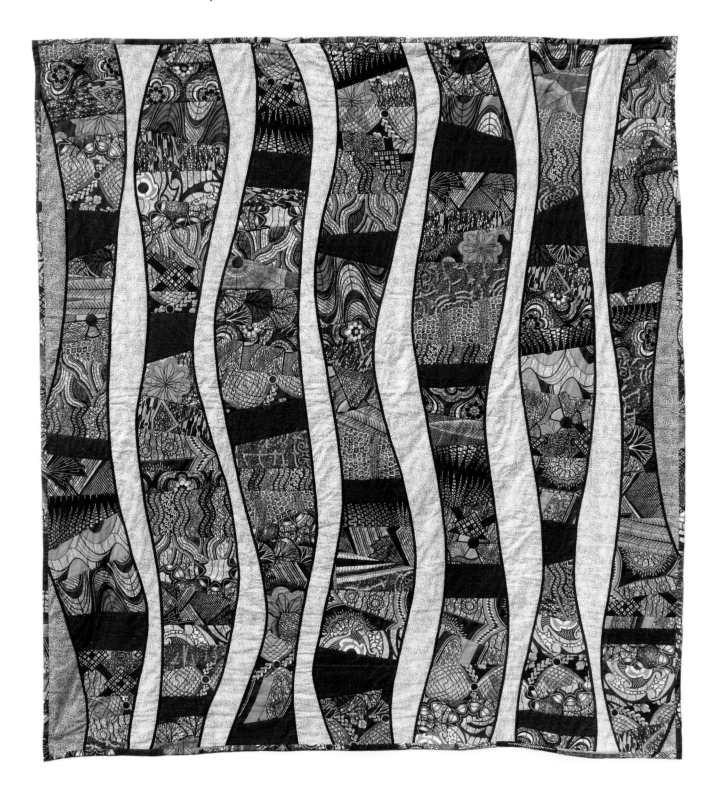

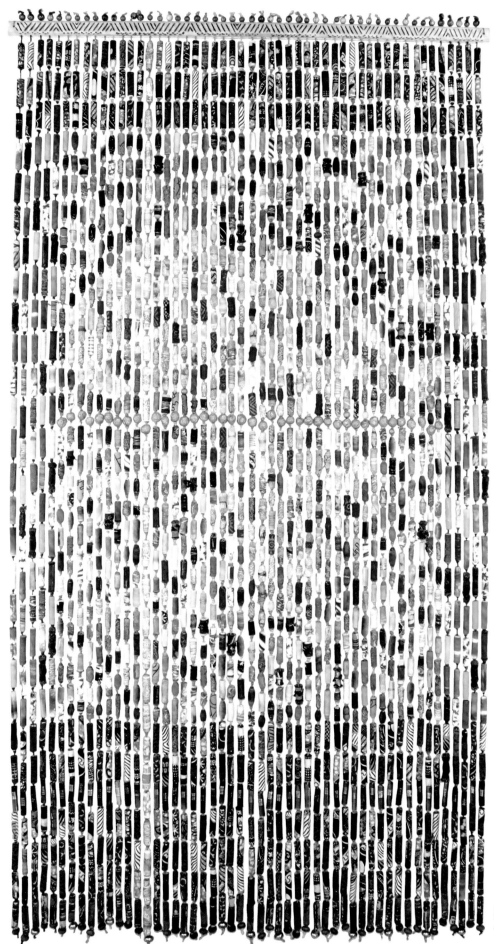

Ushanga,
190 x 102 cm

Helen Conway *Guguletu*

As my pile of African fabrics grows ever higher, I joke that Magie is practising *juju* on me. The lawyer in me tends towards order and convention. But my artistic side craves surprise and rebellion: just like the bold, improvisational style of an African woman wrapped in wax print. Abandoning order isn't easy at first, but once you start, the freedom is irresistible.

Guguletu,
125 x 92 cm

Carole Kokinis *James and Zoe's Safari*

Sewing – patchwork, quilting and appliqué, by hand or machine – is the fabric of my life. I've always loved the use of colour and motif in Kente cloth from Ghana. In this quilt, I've built upon Kente's strip-weaving tradition and adapted it to the block tradition of patchwork. Using wax print fabrics was an enjoyable new challenge for me, so I tried to let their vibrancy complement the overall design.

James and Zoe's Safari,
165 x 143 cm

Alison Farmer *Vitambara & Africa I*

Africa was my home for sixteen years. I love the bustle of the cities, the solitude of the bush and the vivid colours of the costumes and fabrics. I met Magie in Nairobi when she was a guest of the Kenya Quilt Guild and she introduced me to strip-woven mud cloth. The result is *Vitambara* (Swahili for 'strips of cloth'), which she included in her 'Under African Skies' exhibition at the Quilters' Guild Museum and Gallery in York. *Africa I* grew out of my South African stash, an inspiring quilt class with Lee Hackman in Zimbabwe, and the remembering process after I'd moved to Eritrea.

Vitambara, 120 x 80 cm

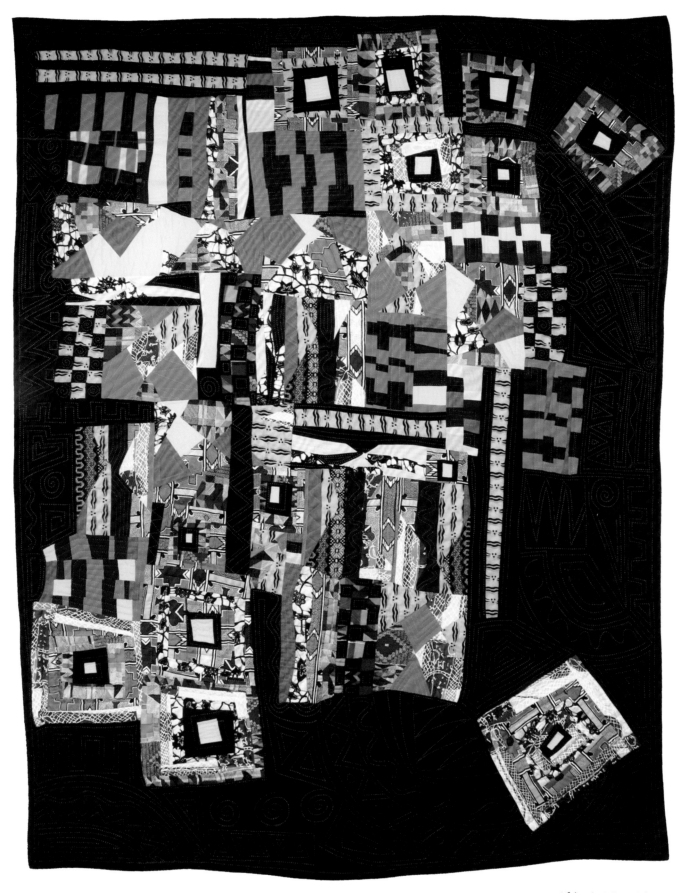

Africa I, 172 x 134 cm

Kate Dowty *Wax Work*

I use fabric, threads and colour to interpret the world around me. *Wax Work* was my contribution to a challenge set by Stitch Witches, a group of Surrey-based quilters. Inspired by the colours and lines of one of Magie's wax print fabrics called *Coin Cascade*, I chopped up an image of the fabric into puzzle pieces. Each Stitch Witch created a block based on their puzzle piece and the colourway of the original fabric. I then reassembled the blocks, merging colour and shape into a cohesive whole.

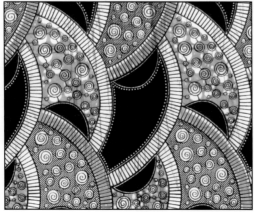

Wax Work, 64 x 81 cm, and its inspiration – the wax print *Coin Cascade*

Margaret Ramsay *Creation Myth*

Creation myths are common in most cultures. My textile interpretation is built around two primitive appliqué figures from my growing collection of vintage world textiles, set off by the colours and forms of African wax print. I've been working with wax print since 1999 when I became Magie's first internet customer. It all seems such a long way from my first wax print – worn by my childhood rag doll.

Creation Myth, 116 x 141 cm

Roselle Abramowitz *Painters' Shirts*

Is there a boundary between function and form, between the clothing we wear and the art we admire? My philosophy is: wear it, hang it on a wall, let it beautify your space. What attracts me to African wax print? The bold colours and designs: each fabric speaks to me in a different, magical way. I feel almost like an interpreter, bringing disparate conversations together into a single statement.

Ann Mayner *Pegs Might Fly*

As a quilter, I like to strive for the unusual, thinking and creating outside of my comfort zone. What could be further out there than a challenge from Magie using a wacky wax print with a clothes-peg motif and the pun 'Pegs Might Fly'?

African art, imagery and costume inspired my Africanised take on Sunbonnet Sue. And I love the bold complexity of the retro wax border fabric, which proved a great starting point for quilting.

Pegs Might Fly,
103 x 71 cm

CPR – Message From My Mother, 160 x 148 cm

Beth Ann St. George
CPR – Message From My Mother & Cups

I try to create without too much cerebral interference: art as meditation. With my fabrics laid out, something was missing. In my stash, I found a 40-year-old piece of Boussac cotton which I'd bought for my mother. I thought of three words: confidence, persistence, resilience. The next day, a truck passed: on its side the words 'CPR Electrical'. When I finished the quilt on the twentieth anniversary of her passing, it felt like a *Message From My Mother*.

Sometimes, the process is more whimsical. I just loved this playful cups fabric. Are they cups of dreams, of fulfilment, or just our morning coffee?

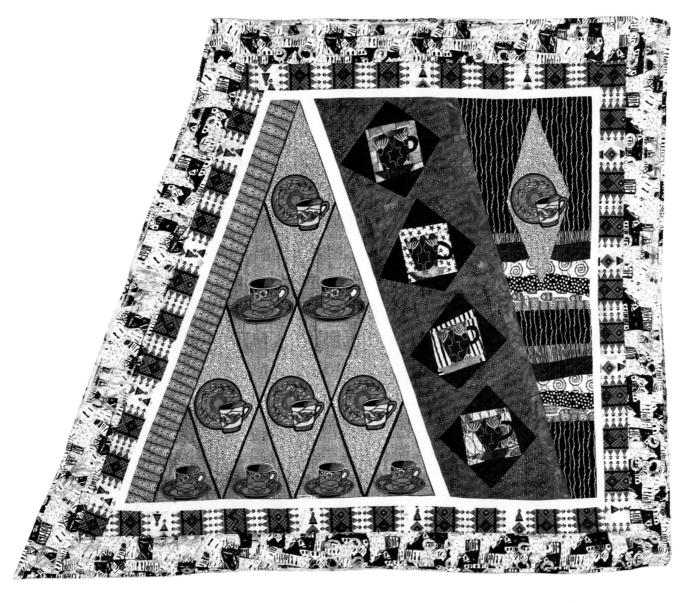

Cups, 158 x 184 cm

New Horizons 'Fabric of a Nation'

The British Museum's 'Fabric of a Nation' exhibition chronicled 50 years of Ghanaian independence through commemorative fabrics.

The New Horizons textile group supported the exhibition when it toured to the Luton Museum.

Stephanie Pettengell
Waxing Waves Green

The shell and wave design of this wax print works perfectly with the cut and stitched wave technique, so we see two fabrics simultaneously: Ghana old and new (50 x 20 cm).

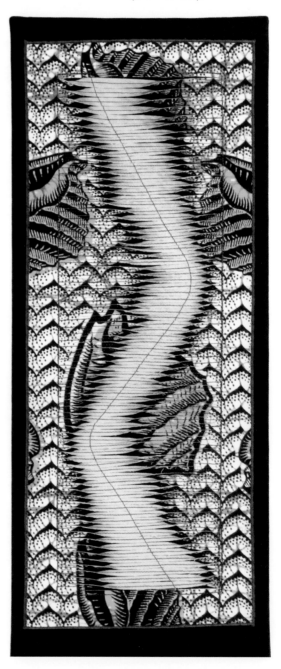

Janice Gunner *Silver Moon*
A wonderful wax print, simply embellished with stitch and appliqué (50 x 25 cm).

Jane Munns *Woven Squares*

I was drawn to the dynamic design and colours of the fabric, leaving the patterned squares to speak for themselves (29 x 25 cm).

Wendy Mose *Spider's Web*

The spider's web is an Adinkra symbol for creativity and wisdom, which is exactly the feeling I got from this symmetrically dotted wax print fabric (26 x 26 cm).

Dorita Smith *Ethel & Max*

I love combining wax print with traditional patchwork designs, where convention might say they shouldn't work. I name my quilts after someone special who is in my thoughts as I sew. *Ethel* is my favourite: I just threw everything in without any real plan.

Max I made as a respite from a black and white quilt – I just needed my wax prints! Cutting and piecing these big, bold patterns can lead almost anywhere. Can you find the table tennis fabric in *Max*?

Ethel, 137 x 137 cm

Max,
141 x 126 cm

Isobel Holland *Cotton Reels*

My design process usually starts with a concept, not with the fabric itself. Wax print is completely different. It has so much presence and personality. I just had to start experimenting, putting prints together to see how they talk to each other. In Africa, wax print speaks for its wearer. So what could be better for a stitcher than a quilt bordered with needles, threads and scissors?

Cotton Reels, 175 x 175 cm

Magie Relph *Flower Stems*

Many quilters feel intimidated by African wax print. They love the colours and designs, but hesitate. 'I can't cut it up,' they plead. Well why not? Patchwork, for me, is all about working with the fabrics: cutting them up and puzzling them back together. That's *Flower Stems*: take same fabric in four colourways, cut up and reassemble – then quilt!

Flower Stems, 125 x 110 cm

About the authors

Magie Relph

Magie Relph is a quilter, textile artist, teacher and author. Since 1984 she has wandered and wondered throughout Africa, studying, documenting and buying African textiles. In the 1990s she opened her battered cardboard suitcase full of wax prints to her quilt group, and her fair trade 'accidental business' – The African Fabric Shop – was born.

Robert Irwin

Robert Irwin has only had malaria once, but he's had Africa in his blood since he was 10. For over 25 years he has travelled, photographed and written passionately about Africa, most recently with his wife Magie, about African textile traditions. He is The African Fabric Shop's web designer and full-time 'Saturday Boy'.

Resources and further reading

Books

Clarke, Duncan, *The Art of African Textiles*, Thunder Bay Press, 1977.

Faber, Paul, *Long Live the President*, KIT Publishers, 2010.

Fauque, Claude and Wollenweber, Otto, *Tissus d'Afrique*, Editions Syros-Alternatives, 1991.

Gillow, John, *African Textiles: Colour and Creativity Across a Continent*, Thames & Hudson, 2003.

Grossfilley, Anne, *L'Afrique des textiles*, Édisud, 2004.

LaGamma, Alisa and Giuntini, Christine, *The Essential Art of African Textiles: Design Without End*, Metropolitan Museum of Art, 2008.

Michel, Serge and Beuret, Michel, *China Safari*, Nation Books, 2009.

Picton, John, *The Art of African Textiles: Technology, Tradition and Lurex*, Barbican Art Gallery & Lund Humphries, 1999.

Picton, John and Mack, John, *African Textiles*, British Museum Press, 1995.

Polakoff, Claire, *African Textiles and Dyeing Techniques*, Routledge & Kegan Paul, 1982.

Spring, Chris, *African Art in Detail*, British Museum Press, 2009.

Storey, Joyce, *Textile Printing*, Thames & Hudson, 1974.

Websites

A Brunnschweiler & Co.: www.abcwax.com

BBC: www.bbc.co.uk

Bharat Textile: www.bharattextile.com

Cha Textiles: www.chatextiles.com

Competition Commission: www.competition-commission.org.uk

Grace's Guide: www.gracesguide.co.uk

Vlisco: www.vlisco.co.uk

Articles, etc.

Boateng, Caroline and Bonney, Emmanuel, 'Textile industry faces gloomy future', *Daily Graphic*, Accra, 2 February 2010.

Castonguay, Sylvie, 'The Modern Tale of Nigerian Wax-Resist Textiles', *World Intellectual Property Organization magazine*, July 2009.

Harrop, Gerald, *Newton Bank Printworks Hyde 1812–2007*, unpublished manuscript.

Heath, Deborah, 'Fashion, Anti-fashion and Heteroglossia in Urban Senegal', *American Ethnologist*, 19(2), 1992.

Launert, Frederika, 'Notes on the Manchester–West African Cotton Trade 1900–39', *TEXT: For the Study of Textile Art, Design & History*, vol 25, winter 2007.

Ryan, Orla, 'Chinese Threat for Ghana's textile firms', *BBC News Online*, 30 August 2006.

Steiner, Christopher B, 'Another Image of Africa: Toward an Ethnohistory of European Cloth Marketed in West Africa, 1873–1960', *Ethnohistory*, 32(2), 1985.

Steinglass, Matt, 'How a Dutch company's batik textiles became the basis of "traditional" West African culture', *Metropolis*, December 2000.

Turlings, Yvette, 'Fashion Makers of Africa', *Radio Netherlands*, 8 April 2002.

Yeboah, Kofi, 'AGI calls on government to salvage textile industry', *Daily Graphic*, Accra, 5 February 2010.

Fabric of a Nation exhibition catalogue, British Museum Press, 2008.

'The Brunnschweiler Story', unidentified and undated trade press.

'The Real Dutch Wax: Vlisco', *New African*, March 2000.